# WORSHIP
# AND
# EVANGELISM

Andy Langford
and
Sally Overby Langford

P.O. Box 189 • Nashville, TN 37202 • Phone (615) 340-7285

ISBN 0-88177-074-4

Library of Congress Catalog Card No. 89-50667

All scriptural quotations are taken from *Hearing the Word: An Inclusive Language Liturgical Lectionary,* produced by St. Stephen and the Incarnation Episcopal Church, Washington, DC, 1982-86. Used by permission.

All excerpts from worship services are taken from *The Book of Services,* published by Abingdon Press, 1985. Used by permission. These also appear in *The United Methodist Hymnal* (United Methodist Publishing House, 1989). All page numbers refer to *The United Methodist Hymnal.*

WORSHIP AND EVANGELISM. Copyright © 1989 by Discipleship Resources. All rights reserved. Printed in the United States of America. No part of this book may be reproduced in any manner whatsoever without written permission except in the case of brief quotations embodied in critical articles or reviews. For information address Discipleship Resources Editorial Offices, P. O. Box 840, Nashville, TN 37202.

DR074B

*To Ann Green and Sarah*

# CONTENTS

Foreword   *vii*

Introduction: Worship and Evangelism   *ix*

1. GETTING PEOPLE TO WORSHIP   1

    Identifying Your Audience   1

    Inviting Persons to Worship   3

    Telling Your Story   6

2. SERVICE OF WORSHIP: ENTRANCE AND PROCLAMATION   11

    Call and Response   11

    Entrance   13

    Proclamation and Response   18

3. SERVICE OF WORSHIP: INVITATIONS AND RESPONSES   23

    Invitations as Catalysts   23

    The Variety of Invitations and Responses   25

4. SERVICE OF WORSHIP: THANKSGIVING WITH COMMUNION AND SENDING FORTH   43

    The Baptismal Covenant   44

    The Lord's Supper   45

    Sending Forth   50

5. THE CHRISTIAN YEAR   55

    Advent/Christmas/Epiphany   56

    Lent/Easter/Pentecost   61

    Ordinary Time    66
    Special Services    68

6. PLANNING FOR WORSHIP AND EVANGELISM    71
    Strong Leadership    71
    Good Teaching    72
    Extensive Plans    74
    Congregational Support    79
    Evaluation and Refinement    80
    Conclusion    80

Bibliography    83

# FOREWORD

United Methodist churches throughout the world are making covenants to grow in ministry and grow in numbers. We believe that church growth will come as a result of our witness and service in the world. We know that churches grow when Christians share their faith stories with persons who are alienated from God or who are not involved in the life of the church. We gain this perspective from reading scripture, from studying the conversion experiences of Christians through the centuries, and from our own personal experience.

We also know that as disciples we must receive new persons in our congregations and avoid judging their faith stories or dismissing their struggle to know God. Thus we help all persons relate to God and develop Christian faith, equipping them and sending them out as disciples of the One who is the Lord of all of life.

We can translate this evangelistic commission into the language of those who study the reasons for church growth. One fruitful way to describe the reasons for church growth is to identify 1) factors that attract persons to the gospel and the church, 2) factors that influence persons to make a commitment to Christ and membership in a congregation, and 3) factors that bond persons in their relationship with Christ and the church.

Each pastor and each lay minister of the gospel knows that there are no snappy solutions, no easy five or ten steps which should result in "x" number of persons attending Sunday morning worship. Yet we can identify factors that focus our prayer and ministry on the pathways to church growth. Pastors of growing churches prefer to rank the factors which contribute to membership growth. Our research shows that the top ten factors are:

1. Vital worship services
2. Fellowship and relational settings
3. Pastor and pastoral functions
4. Sharply targeted ministries

5. Community/world Outreach
6. Christian education
7. Growth posture/planning
8. Physical facilities and location
9. Lay leadership/involvement
10. Evangelism activities

This series, Pathways to Church Growth, includes books and booklets containing practical suggestions for ministry related to these ten factors. The resources are written by leaders in the church and by successful pastors of growing churches. This book by Andy and Sally Overby Langford describes the crucial ways that your worship service must function as a catalyst for evangelism. Each aspect of your worship service is given added vitality if you design the event so that persons have the chance to respond in faithful discipline and with acts of mercy in their communities.

Too often, persons concerned about worship dismiss the ultimate goal of worship: the offering of grace. Too often, persons concerned about evangelism dismiss the primary location of evangelism: services of corporate worship. This book is one attempt to explore the relationship between worship and evangelism.

In today's church, both worship and evangelism are critically needed—not for the survival of the institutional church but for women, men, and children in need of God's love. Who are these people who need God? We are those people! We are busy people, trying to make a living, experiencing joy and distress in relationships, attempting to do good and often sinning. We are people harassed by money problems, family claims, and childhood, teenage, young adult, mid-life, and elderly crises. We are people hurt, lonely, hungry, and dying. We are people who have made it for another week and need to make it for still another week. We are people spiritually excited and spiritually empty. We are people coming to worship and hoping that God will be there.

I invite you to join together with Christians everywhere in redoubling your ministry and commitment to a growing church. Tell your story about what God has done for you, and encourage people in your community who want to know how Christ makes a difference in our lives.

EZRA EARL JONES
General Secretary
General Board of Discipleship
The United Methodist Church

# Introduction: Worship and Evangelism

The night was cold and damp. The revival was in its fourth night. A sudden snowstorm had kept many people away. A small mountain congregation bravely sang a few hymns, quietly heard the Word read and proclaimed, and fervently offered prayer. Junior had come that night with his wife Maxine; he did not believe or belong. But on this night Junior was present, he was a part of the congregation, and God's love reached out to him. Although crippled by disease, Junior arose and came forward on his crutches. Three weeks later, we baptized Junior in the Linville River.

\* \* \* \* \*

Suzie grew up Lutheran. Baptized and confirmed in a Lutheran congregation, she had been an active Christian as a youth. But times changed and she had become inactive. Marriage, work, and young children kept her away from church. Then after an invitation, Suzie began to work with the United Methodist youth. The leadership was important for her and to be a good role model, she started attending worship. For almost one year she was faithful in attendance. Throughout the year, we talked together about God and the church. After much conversation and thoughtful reflection, Suzie came forward one Sunday to reaffirm her baptismal vows.

\* \* \* \* \*

Sadie was a saint of the church. She never missed Sunday school, Sunday morning worship, or United Methodist Women. She attended the weekly Bible study group and regularly visited the congregation's shut-ins. One Sunday, following a sermon about prayer, Sadie came forward, knelt at the chancel rail, and rededicated herself to God. It was not her first dedication, but it was an important landmark in her spiritual pilgrimage.

\* \* \* \* \*

Three different people. Three different United Methodist congregations. Three different events. Yet in each case, an individual heard God offering grace in worship and offered himself or herself back to God.

Throughout the history of the church, worship and evangelism have been closely connected. On the day of Pentecost, Peter preached, and three thousand people heard the good news, repented, and were baptized. Day after day, the early Christians gathered to praise God and to share the Lord's Supper. And day after day, the Lord added numbers to this close-knit worshiping congregation (Acts 2).

And so it is in today's church. Bringing about numerical church growth is never the focus of a congregation's worship service. Yet, whenever Christians gather to worship God and to respond to God's love for them, growth takes place. Sometimes this growth is numerical. If unchurched people like Junior are present at our worship services, they may hear God's call to them, and they will respond by deciding to follow Jesus, to be baptized, and to join the congregation. At all times, the growth is spiritual. Christians, like Suzie, who have lost their enthusiasm and zeal for the gospel, may find within our worship services a new sense of call and commitment. They will renew the vows that were made at their baptism. Other Christians are like Sadie. They are active church members. And yet, God's call still comes to them. They too can find in the midst of Christian worship continual strength and energy to grow in their love for God and their neighbors.

Worship is when the church gathers to hear the Word, to baptize, to eat and drink, to pray, and to become the body of Christ. Throughout the history of the church universal, and particularly within our own Wesleyan tradition, worship affords the church the opportunity to praise God and has been the means of grace through which the prevenient, justifying, and sanctifying grace of God saves. In these moments, the church remembers who it is, rehearses its story, and becomes a new creation. God becomes present and the community experiences the reality of God to the end that God is glorified and humanity is sanctified.

"Evangelism is witness. It is one beggar telling another beggar where to get food. Christians do not offer out of their bounty. They have no bounty. They are simply guests at their Master's table and, as evangelists, they call others too." (D.T. Niles, "Venite Adoremus II" *World's Student Christian Federation Prayer Book*, 1938, pp. 105ff)

Worship and evangelism are closely related because they both reflect the same foundational dynamic: call and response. Throughout the Bible and Christian tradition, God called persons to repent of their sins, to lead just lives, and to share this message with all creation. Through a burning

# Introduction

bush, God called Moses to go to Pharaoh and set the people free. Moses heard and went. Jesus called Peter beside the Sea of Galilee. Peter followed. God spoke to John Wesley at a society meeting at Aldersgate, and the Wesleyan revival began. God also calls people today, and they respond with joy and thanksgiving.

Call and response are central to the church's ministry. Pastors, musicians, and whole congregations call persons to know and trust God. Individuals and whole communities respond. Leaders tell the story, and persons listen and follow. God convicts persons of their sins, and some repent. God justifies persons alienated from God, and some become children of the Almighty again. God sanctifies persons, and they move toward maturity. In each case, *metanoia* (conversion, or reorientation) occurs. Conversion is more than just a good experience of self-fulfillment; God saves persons!

Such conversion is complex. As witnessed in two important books, *The Mystery and Meaning of Christian Conversion* by George E. Morris and *Conversions* edited by Hugh Kerr and John Mulder, no one pattern fits everyone. Conversion may be both instantaneous and gradual, personal and corporate, and the result of a single crisis and a long process. Conversion involves a constellation of factors, with many stars, configurations, and visions. Yet, what is common in all conversions is that each is initiated by God's call and a human response. Most often, this encounter occurs in worship.

In today's church, as in the church throughout the ages, worship is the primary event in which persons and communities hear and respond to God's call. Through worship as a means of grace, God convicts, justifies, and sanctifies. As John Wesley said: "There is but one scriptural way wherein we receive inward grace—through the outward means [the Word of God read, proclaimed and heard, the sacraments rightly taught and practiced, prayer, and Christian fellowship] which God hath ordained" (Telford, *Letters III*; pp. 366-67). Worship is the primary evangelistic act of the church.

The contemporary leaders of the church know that worship is the primary evangelistic act of the church. Lyle Schaller has stated that church growth depends on worship. Likewise, Kennon Callahan in *Twelve Keys to an Effective Church* states that worship is a key to church growth. He writes, "Now, more unchurched persons [74% of first contacts] find their way first to the service of worship" (p. 24). Pastors at the 1986 St. Louis Convocation on growing United Methodist congregations agreed that worship is the primary entry point of new persons into the community of faith. Without effective evangelistic worship the church dies; with effective evangelistic worship the church lives.

As we will show in this book, effective worship is evangelistic. This meeting with God is not composed of manipulative gimmicks or frightening scare tactics that force persons into a relationship with God. Worship that is shaped by the Word of God, led by sensitive pastors, musicians, and others, appropriate to the gathered congregation, and open to the presence of the Holy Spirit is evangelistic. The goal of worship is not to be ritually correct or emotionally manipulative; true worship effects a new relationship between God and the congregation. In worship God convicts, justifies, and sanctifies.

> Jesus went through all the towns and villages, teaching in their synagogues and proclaiming the Gospel of the Kingdom, healing every disease and every infirmity. When Jesus saw the crowds, he had compassion for them, because they were harassed and helpless, like sheep without a shepherd. Then he said to his disciples, "The harvest is plentiful, but the workers are few; so ask the Lord of the harvest to send out workers into the harvest field" (Matthew 9:35-38).

Pastors, musicians, worship and evangelism committees, and whole congregations must all respond to the needs of our age. The harvest is plentiful and laborers are needed. The intention of this book is to help those working in the vineyard plan worship services, every Sunday throughout the year, that offer God's good news to everyone. "Pray therefore the Lord of the harvest to send out laborers into the harvest" (Matthew 9:38).

# 1. GETTING PEOPLE TO WORSHIP

A large stained glass window illuminates Duke Memorial United Methodist Church in Durham, North Carolina. The window portrays John Wesley standing on his father's tomb at Epworth. From this position, Wesley preaches to a crowd of people. Wesley had been forbidden to preach to his "home" church, and parish members had stopped coming to Epworth's worship services. In this scene, Wesley takes the gospel to the people in a setting other than the Epworth sanctuary!

Many people in your community are not in church on Sunday morning. They are not comfortable coming into your sanctuary at the traditional worship hour. While you wait inside for them to come to you, they are waiting outside for you to come to them. The result is that people do not hear and are not able to respond to the Word of God.

This chapter details how your congregation can encourage its members to attend worship regularly. At the same time, your congregation must make the initial contacts to encourage visitors to attend worship. Three basic steps will make your work possible: identifying your audience and its needs, inviting persons to worship, and telling your story. John Wesley took the gospel to the people at graveyards, street corners, coal fields, prisons, and deserted buildings. The circuit riders traveled miles to where people lived. No less can be expected of us.

## Identifying Your Audience

On the Day of Pentecost, the Holy Spirit descended upon the disciples and gave them the gift of tongues (Acts 2). With this gift of tongues, the disciples preached to the people gathered in Jerusalem in their own native languages. The whole of Jerusalem heard the gospel clearly.

Today's church is not so fortunate. Your worshiping congregation usually reflects only a small part of the whole congregation and certainly a small percentage of the whole community. In order for the gospel to be heard, your congregation must first identify to whom it is speaking.

Identify who is present in your congregation on Sunday morning and specify their needs. Are they older adults, families with children, or both? And ask: Does your worship encourage those members to attend worship regularly? For example, for your older adults, are there enough large print bulletins and an adequate sound system? Do you provide van service for those unable to drive? Do you meet the needs of families with young children by offering children's bulletins and nursery care?

Warren Hartman in his book *Five Audiences* identifies five distinct types of groups present in most congregations: fellowship, traditional, study, social concerns, and multiple interest groups. Your planning for worship must begin with an identification of the different groups in your congregation and their needs. For example, if your congregation is predominantly a group of persons who gather for fellowship (most congregations fit into this category), are there multiple occasions for celebrating and sharing in your worship? And what about other groups? Do you also offer multiple worship opportunities to provide for those who desire traditional worship, informative worship, and varied worship? For example, the social concerns group in your local church may well seek a service that includes explicit references—for penance and action—to combat the nuclear arms race, world hunger, or child abuse.

Yet, effective worship does not end when you meet the needs of your members. True worship allows God to meet the needs of all people. Do not limit your concern to your members who are currently active in worship. If you focus, for example, only on the large number of older adults in your congregation and their needs, you will eliminate younger adults from your worship services. Your congregation must continually ask, "Who is our neighbor?"

Every congregation must discover the whole community that it serves. Your church might take a religious census of the community using "Religious Census" resources from Discipleship Resources. Or, you might take a telephone survey. These efforts will be helpful, but they are limited by their impersonal character. Many people are weary of being surveyed.

The most effective way to identify new persons is by personal contact. Parishes are now defined not by geography but by relationships. Let the members of your congregation think of those individuals who work beside them, who live near them, or who are related to them. If these people are not active in another congregation, they need the grace God offers in worship.

Once new people have been identified, try to identify their needs, hopes, interests, dreams, and aspirations. What do you offer in worship that meets people where they are? Said negatively, are you doing things in worship that block people's participation? It is not sufficient simply to find unchurched people and invite them to come to worship as you have always done worship. Your congregation must be more willing to shape itself in ways that respond to the deepest needs of those who come to it.

One group of people your church might not be reaching is the group of young adults aged 23 to 40, who are sometimes called the "baby-boomers." Of all these persons born since World War II only 40 percent belong to any religious congregation. Most active in congregations are those couples with children, followed by married couples without children, and then singles. Look for these different persons in your community. Ask them about their needs and concerns. The couples with children may request that your church involve children in the worship services and a program to involve children in worship might follow. Couples without children are often looking for a fellowship group; a time for building fellowship within the congregation might need to be a part of your worship service. Singles, living on wholly different schedules from others, may want a Saturday evening worship service that is relaxed, informal, and spontaneous.

A second group of people often overlooked by our churches is found in resident ethnic communities. The people of First United Methodist Church in Rapid City, South Dakota, discovered Native-American, Japanese, and Hispanic persons within their community. Because of time and effort on the part of church members, this congregation now provides worship in three languages and advertises for worship in four languages.

## Inviting Persons to Worship

Clay United Methodist Church in South Bend, Indiana, gives calling cards to all members. On the front is the church's logo "Come grow with us," along with the times of Sunday school and worship. The back of the card includes a small map locating the church, the pastor's name and phone, the hours of youth ministry, and most important, a line for a member's name and phone number. Members of the congregation distribute the cards, signed with their names, to their friends and neighbors.

Having identified the persons both within and beyond your congregation and their needs, how do you invite them to join you? One major new approach is the *Growth Plus Worship Attendance Crusade* from Discipleship Resources. It shows how to operate and publicize a worship crusade. The major ways to include more persons in worship are by personal invitation, adapting the time and place of worship, providing transportation, and offering better parking for vehicles.

## PERSONAL INVITATIONS

At Linville United Methodist Church in the North Carolina mountains, Edith Webb won disciples for Christ. Each week Edith called on the members of the church to see how they were doing. Visitors received a phone call and visit. The sick received flowers, and the shut-ins received cards. Nobody slipped through Edith's fingers.

The single most effective tool for gathering people for worship is personal contact. A phone call, a face-to-face conversation, or a card tells persons that they are important and welcome. The options are varied: A church member offers a neighbor a ride to worship; a choir member encourages a friend to join the choir; a child invites a classmate to come hear a children's sermon; a patient in the hospital shares a sermon tape with a roommate.

Many congregations encourage invitations to worship by designating one Sunday a month as "Visitors' Sunday." The worship service is adapted to make visitors feel especially welcome. A coffee hour following worship enables visitors to meet church members and staff.

Starting new choirs is another solid way to increase church attendance. Every church needs a new choir. Start a children's choir, a men's chorus, a youth choir, a handbell choir, or an orchestra. The key to using these groups effectively is visibility. Let the new choirs participate in worship each month, if not more frequently. At a United Methodist church in Puerto Rico, four new choirs were begun and each one sang once a month. Attendance increased. Everyone knows what happens to worship attendance when the children sing!

Again, the most effective tool for gathering people for worship is personal contact. Warm and open invitations by friends, family, and neighbors will gather people together. Your congregation should have a plan for increasing and deepening its personal contact with others.

But what about other ways to invite persons to worship?

## ADAPTING THE TIME AND PLACE OF WORSHIP

In a suburb of San Francisco, a local congregation extended its ministry to a whole group of overlooked people. On Sunday morning at

# Getting People to Worship 5

11:00, in the private dining room of a local cafeteria, young adults gathered for coffee and pastries. Some had eaten breakfast beforehand; others would brunch later. After thirty minutes of gathering, people sat at tables for eight, and a guitarist distributed song sheets. Singing began. Copies of a Bible story were passed out. A young pastor outlined the story and then directed discussions. At 1:00 P.M., the whole company sang a benediction.

Your church must begin to meet the needs of people for whom Sunday morning is not convenient and perhaps your church sanctuary is not inviting. Your congregation should plan to begin at least one new service of worship, if it intends to share the gospel more widely. Examples are numerous. Plan an early Sunday morning worship service for families with young children or for people who wish to spend Sunday at the lake. Schedule Saturday or Sunday evening services, which are popular among single adults. Plan worship on a weekday morning for people who must work on Sunday or the late night shift. On Wednesday evenings have a supper and time of worship for families. A variety of options will help your outreach.

Yet, more than time changes are necessary. Many people are not comfortable being in the church sanctuary. In response, you may offer worship in other settings, including the fellowship hall, chapel, classroom, garden (depending on the weather), park, retreat center, street corners, fields, apartment building lobbies, homes, and parking lots. Robert Schuller began his effective ministry at a drive-in theater!

Now, if you have scheduled worship at times and places to meet people (rather than having people change to meet you), how else can you invite them to worship?

## PROVIDE BETTER PARKING

At a large New York church, teenagers of the congregation provide a valet service. Persons may drive up to a side door and have the youth park their cars. With graciousness, people are welcomed to worship. At Royal Oaks United Methodist Church, a small congregation, attendance increased when the members paved the church parking lot.

Americans today are closely tied to their cars. Drive-ins and drive-thrus are popular. If people find parking difficult, they may drive away. Be sure that your church has multiple entrances. Use a parking director to direct traffic, give directions, and assist persons with special needs. Persons with handicapping conditions often need parking under a shelter. And be certain that you provide adequate parking space. A downtown Nashville congregation purchased a parking garage just to be sure that safe and convenient parking is available.

## OFFER TRANSPORTATION

In Cherokee, North Carolina, the United Methodist church provides van service for the Cherokee people. When asked why she became United Methodist, a woman replied, "Because the United Methodists came and picked me up on Sunday morning." This is evangelism.

The church must go out and seek people who cannot be present at worship otherwise. Your community has persons with handicapping conditions, elderly persons in rest homes, persons without transportation, and children without active church families. Many of these persons are waiting to come to church, and it is up to your church to bring them into the community.

## Telling Your Story

The Weld House is a small boardinghouse down the road from Altamont United Methodist Church. Guests from across the country stay there throughout the summer. One summer, the Altamont congregation placed a small card in every room telling the time and place of worship. And often, guests of the Weld House came to worship.

Every survey of persons and needs overlooks many people. No amount of personal invitation and other ways of inviting persons into worship will reach everyone in the community. How can you tell your whole community about worship? There are four major ways to tell your story: advertising, providing signs, making your setting attractive, and using the electronic media.

## ADVERTISING

In central Florida, a United Methodist church advertises its worship in a wide variety of ways. Ads are placed on television and radio, on bill-

# Getting People to Worship

boards, in the yellow pages, and even on city buses. All the residents of that town know about that particular United Methodist church. They know who the pastor is, when the church worships, and that they are welcome!

In our contemporary culture, few people will come to your church because of your denominational label. Rather, they will come because you have reached out to them and have told them what you offer. Many tools are available to help you tell your story to the people of your community.

Make use of all the media available: television, radio, telephone answering programs, flyers, posters, billboards, motel message boards, and bumper stickers. Place your church name and times of the worship services in the yellow pages. Advertise in newspapers, but not on the religion page. Place your newspaper ads on the sports pages or classified pages.

The quality of such advertising should be dramatic. One example includes a photograph of pallbearers and a coffin with the copy: "Will it take six strong men to bring you back into the church?" Another has a picture of Jesus with the caption: "You can't meet God's gift to women in a singles bar" (*New York Times,* December 27, 1987, p. F4). Appoint a church publicity manager who will send weekly press releases of church happenings to your local newspapers.

Direct mail advertising is an effective tool for telling your story. Check your yellow pages to locate companies in your area that will provide mailing lists of people in zip codes nearest to you. Some churches send letters of welcome to new residents in their neighborhoods. Others use the mailing lists to contact single or older adults.

Experience has shown that colorful brochures draw more attention to a church than long letters from the pastor. And several mailings spread out over a period of time work better than a one-time mailing. Experiment and see what works best for your church.

If you need professional help in designing your direct mail advertising, you may want to contact Specialized Ministries Center (85 Welsh Road, Maple Glen, PA 19002) about its Direct Mail Consultation Service. Also, Jim Lavender, a United Methodist pastor in Richmond, Virginia, has organized "The Direct Mail Kit," which is full of helpful hints about what kind and color of paper to use for your mailings, what times of year to contact people, and what information to include in your mailings. (For more information on the kit, write Discovery United Methodist Church, 2627 Pleasant Run Drive, Richmond, VA 23233.) You may also encourage visitors by distributing the leaflet *An Invitation from Your United Methodist Friends* from Discipleship Resources.

Mail out your bulletins or church newspapers weekly. A highly effective tool for increased church attendance among members is a weekly bulletin, which arrives on Friday or Saturday and includes the scripture and sermon topic for that Sunday. Use this method to build up excitement for Sunday.

Professionally prepared programs can help you with your publicity. The United Methodist Publishing House has an extensive "Catch the Spirit" program. Net Resource Center (5001 Avenue N., Lubbock, TX 79412) has seasonal radio spots called "Got a Minute?" that are to be used at special seasons of the church year. The center also has sixty-second radio "Bright Spots" to be used on a daily basis throughout the year. For television, Net Resource Center provides "Magnetic TV Commercials" that are personalized for each congregation. Discipleship Resources has radio spots prepared by the Growth Plus office at the General Board of Discipleship.

One new and provocative method of advertising is telemarketing. Congregations in New Mexico, Virginia, Illinois, and Indiana have all used a program of calling thousands of persons to discover several hundred open to visiting a congregation (10 percent will respond to a new church, 5 percent to an existing congregation). For more information, write Norm Whan of the Quaker Church, P.O. Box 1607, Whittier, CA 90609-1607.

Remember that you are not *selling* a product, for grace cannot be sold at any price. Rather, you are offering a free gift of immeasurable worth. Grace is not ours to hide under a bushel, but ours to proclaim as a light in the darkness. Let us do it boldly!

## PROVIDING SIGNS

At a Nashville, Tennessee, church, numerous signs welcome visitors and members alike. The street signs direct the flow of traffic. Parking spaces reserved for visitors are right in front of the sanctuary. A directional board indicates where the nursery, classrooms, offices, and sanctuary are. And all hallways have clear directional signs.

Once worship has been adapted by time and place to the needs of the congregation and others, you must help people find your church. You must be aggressively accessible!

Imagine yourself as a visitor. Can you locate your church building and discover where to park and which door to enter? Signs on surrounding

# Getting People to Worship

roads should give directions to the church's doors and hours of worship. Your church should have at least one major sign that gives the time of worship, the name of your pastor(s), and a phone number to call for assistance and information. With regard to the phone number, one church has a shut-in member with a friendly telephone voice, who finds this ministry her vital contribution to the outreach of the congregation.

Access to the building must be available to persons with handicapping conditions, and signs should indicate points of access. A ramp for persons in wheelchairs is a visible sign of welcome. Elevators are indispensable. And Braille signs indicate an openness to persons with visual handicaps.

Once the building has been found, signs should indicate where its rooms are, including the sancutary, nursery, and restrooms. A final note on signs: Keep signs repaired, painted, and timely. Nothing speaks more boldly of a congregation's self-image than the signs it places around itself. See *Ushering and Greeting* from Discipleship Resources for more help.

## MAKING YOUR SETTING ATTRACTIVE

At a rural mountain church in Altamont, North Carolina, Don Wiseman attends to the church grounds. Each spring, he plants new flowers around the building. Throughout the summer he cuts the grass. And at Advent, he trims the frazier firs and places wreaths on the church doors. His attention to the place of worship attracts people to the church.

Outdoor settings should catch the eye. Plant flowers and design attractive landscaping. During Advent, put wreaths on your doors and set up an outdoor crèche. Set up a large cross during Lent and use bright colored streamers and windsocks during Easter and Pentecost. And always be sure that the entrances to your church are uncluttered and vistas to the front doors are clear. Make it impossible for persons not to find the sanctuary.

## USING THE ELECTRONIC MEDIA

At Duke Chapel in Durham, North Carolina, the weekly worship service is televised for the patients of Duke Hospital. In a small South Carolina mill town, worship is heard each week on the local radio station. And in Shreveport, Louisana, First United Methodist Church televises its worship hour.

Congregations use the gifts of television and radio to recall members and draw others. Every congregation has shut-ins and inactives who may tune in. Every community has persons who need to be reminded of grace.

Audio and video resources may be used. Audio and video equipment and tapes are now readily available, and your church can make tapes and distribute them for wider circulation.

To be effective, these media must be used to offer grace. Each service that is broadcast must offer comfort and strength to those who suffer and need God's help. Invitations should be offered for persons to become more active in your congregation. And resources for additional help should be mentioned.

Identifying your audience, inviting persons to worship, and telling your story depend on the wise use of your church's resources. Budget money for printing, postage, gas, and tapes. Assign both staff and laypersons to do this work. And remember that prayer must undergird all that you do. The methods you use will be successful only when your congregation is willing to commit its time, talents, money, and prayers to the task. And such an investment of resources will have the highest return of any program of your church.

# 2. SERVICE OF WORSHIP: ENTRANCE AND PROCLAMATION

People are gathering for worship; they are coming together to be in the presence of God. They are not coming to witness good worship, to sing the classic hymns, to hear a finely prepared sermon, or to listen to a choral anthem. Rather, through words, signs, and actions, they want to experience a new relationship with God. Every child, woman, and man present needs the grace of God.

## Call and Response

The heart of every service of worship must be call and response. God's call to each person must be proclaimed clearly, and each person must be enabled to respond to that call.

The model of call and response for worship in The United Methodist Church is found in the 1984 *Book of Services* (these services are also those included in the new *The United Methodist Hymnal*). These services, approved by the 1984 General Conference, offer a unified pattern that is biblical, Wesleyan, and ecumenical. In each service the Bible is preeminent. Each reflects an Arminian emphasis that demands personal and corporate response to God. And each demonstrates a consensus about worship found by many denominations.

The fundamental pattern in these services, which is also followed in this book, is a dynamic interplay between call and response. Unlike earlier models of worship that were linear and static, this pattern involves a constant dialogue between leaders and people and between God and the congregation. Every act of worship is a call, and is then followed by a response. In turn, the response becomes a further call to a deeper response.

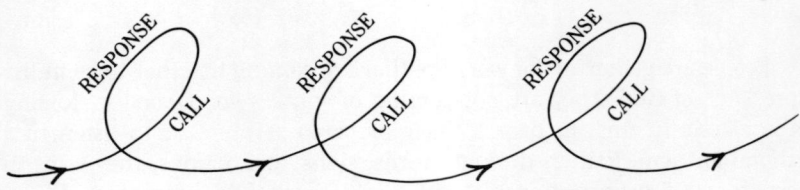

For example, the Word of God read and proclaimed is a call for response. The response may be Holy Communion, which then becomes a call for service to the world. As a whole, the pattern reveals both a unity of intention and a decisive flow.

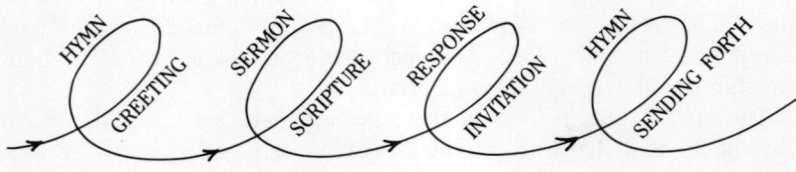

Let us now see how call and response may operate in a service of worship.

## Entrance

At First United Methodist Church in Gainesville, Georgia, the worship begins in the "great hall." The hall stands across from the sanctuary and

# Entrance and Proclamation 13

provides a large gathering space for people to meet and visit. Visitors are welcomed and friends reunited. This gathering makes the people one.

In the "Entrance" of worship, the diversity of persons becomes one body. Persons move from their private realms into a corporate community. While this can happen in many ways, effective worship will not begin until bridges are built. The main thing members and visitors remember about worship is the friendliness or graciousness of the whole congregation. Gathering is the first aspect of "Entrance."

## GATHERING

At West Nashville United Methodist Church, the gathering begins the worship service. As persons enter the front doors and come out of Sunday school classes, the sanctuary becomes a noisy, busy place. Children shake hands with older adults. Friends catch up on the week's news. And the worship leaders quickly resolve last-minute hitches. Worship has begun.

Welcoming people is the most critical aspect of the gathering. Your laypersons and clergy must welcome everyone present, including members and visitors, children and youth. A smile, a handshake, a touch, and a hug make people feel welcome. Remember the biblical images of hospitality. The Old Testament narratives remind us that because God welcomes the stranger, the alien, and the traveler, God's people must do likewise. The stories of Jesus at the wedding feast, at the house of Mary and Martha, with Simon the Pharisee, with Zacchaeus, and at Emmaus all testify to God's being the host of the banquet, even when others think they are! The church is, after all, the house of God!

Greeters should be present at every entrance to the church, and they should be chosen because of their warm, sincere, thoughtful, and helpful qualities. Ask greeters to serve for a month or six weeks so that they will recognize visitors and members. Greeters should wear nametags. They may give nametags, visitor ribbons, or flowers to newcomers. University Park United Methodist Church in Denver, Colorado, presents carnations to all first-time visitors. Or consider giving nametags to all members, as a United Methodist congregation in Dublin, Ohio, does. In addition, greeters may offer visitors a church brochure or other literature, such as a copy of *The Upper Room* devotional magazine.

The following "Greeter's Card" is a sample of what may be used to prepare your greeters.

> **Greeters**
>
> - Wear your nametag.
> - Greet everyone, both members and visitors.
> - Tell your name.
> - Ask the other person's name.
> - Make the other person feel welcome and comfortable.
> - Ask if there are special needs.
> - Give visitors a church brochure and *The Upper Room* magazine.
> - Introduce the visitor to an usher, or
> - Escort the visitor to a seat.
> - Introduce the visitor to others seated nearby.

The greeting of persons reminds your congregation of God's love.

The seating of persons is important. Avoid having the congregation too scattered by roping off back or side sections or pews. When worship becomes too crowded, schedule additional worship services. Offer everyone the opportunity to be seated by a greeter or usher. Place people next to other people, not on an empty pew. Guide visitors to seats next to people with similar interests. For example, seat a young couple with children next to another young couple with children, or next to someone who lives in their apartment complex. Enable persons with handicapping conditions to be seated without drawing attention to them. Finally, and most important, the ushers and greeters should introduce persons to those with whom they sit.

Announcements are most appropriately given at the gathering time. In addition to making announcements about the activities of the church, announce birthdays, anniversaries, weddings, graduations, and achievements. Rather than having your visitors stand or raise their hands and introduce themselves, let those who sit next to visitors introduce them to the congregation. And finally, give directions about worship, which will relieve confusion later in the service. For example, tell how Communion will be served and who is invited to receive it.

Registration of attendance is a necessary tool for worship and evangelism. A comprehensive registration program, when fully implemented, will prove to be a vital link in your congregation's worship. For help, order the booklet *Taking Attendance* from Discipleship Resources.

# Entrance and Proclamation

Now, with the congregation gathered, named, welcomed, and registered, the pastor or other worship leader should set the tone of the service by making a brief statement about the focus of worship that day.

## BULLETINS

A young couple visited the small United Methodist congregation at a crossroads in Durham County. Members greeted them at the door and apologized for not having bulletins. The church was not big enough to have a copying machine. Yet, following a worship service that was led by announcement alone, the young couple complimented the student pastor on the worship service: "We watched and listened to you and we just followed your directions."

Before your worship proceeds, step back just a moment and consider how you lead your congregation through the worship service. Many congregations could eliminate weekly worship bulletins that overload a congregation with a rigid order and details it does not need to know.

Many persons in the pew would prefer a service without worship bulletins. Bulletins may be distributed and include announcements and church information. Yet the basic pattern of hearing and responding to God in worship may be freer and more spontaneous if led by announcement. The leaders need to know the details, but those in the congregation do not. When persons face each other and do not try to keep up with a printed text, the whole dynamic of worship shifts.

If you decide that your congregation must have a weekly worship bulletin, make your bulletin easy to use. Clear page layout is critical. Study *Designing the Sunday Bulletin* by David Wiltse. Within the bulletin, include the following items that make the bulletin "friendly" to the person in the pew:

- name of church
- denomination
- address
- time of worship
- greeters' names
- church phone (including area code)
- home phone of pastor(s) and staff
- name of pastor(s) and staff
- location of hymns (in which book)
- location of acts of worship (in which book)
- the scripture lesson (including page number if pew Bibles are available)

If your congregation includes persons with visual handicaps, provide large-print bulletins by enlarging a bulletin on a copying machine.

## GREETING

> The grace of the Lord Jesus Christ be with you.
> *And also with you.*
> The risen Christ is with us.
> *Praise the Lord!*

The greeting is an exchange between the pastor or worship leader and the people, affirming that God is present.

## HYMN OF PRAISE

A young woman recently joined Belmont United Methodist Church. When asked why she had chosen to join this congregation, her immediate answer was: the music. The same was true in Wesley's day. Methodism was born in song. The Methodist revival was accompanied by a revival of congregational singing. It is rightly debated whether John's sermons or Charles' hymns were more crucial in the Wesleyan revival.

Music, along with preaching, is a key to effective worship and evangelism. Through music, your congregation offers God its prayers and praise. Because of music, your congregation hears the Word afresh and is able to make new faith commitments.

An emphasis on choirs and professional leadership will not necessarily improve the quality of your worship or evangelism, and may in fact make the congregation more passive. Effective music depends on congregational participation. Teach your congregation how to sing and help it sing well.

First, discover what your congregation wants to sing by doing a hymn survey. Build on your congregation's repertoire rather than start with a clean slate. Second, with a hymn repertoire in hand, your pastor, musicians, and the worship planning team must choose hymns that enhance the worship that day. Planning ensures that the worship will include a mix of familiar and new hymns appropriate to the service.

Third, and expecially with the opening hymn of praise, let your people sing the hymns and songs they love. The spectrum should be wide, ranging from classical hymns to contemporary spiritual choruses. But by

# Entrance and Proclamation

using the people's repertoire, you demonstrate that you trust your people and respect their spiritual pilgrimage and their need to express their faith through music. New hymnody must be introduced slowly, carefully, and with significant preparation.

Fourth, help your people sing their hymns and songs with firm instrumental leadership. Encourage your musical accompanist to guide the people. Teach new music in advance. Use the musicians in your midst instead of using paid outsiders or taped music.

Fifth, firm vocal leadership strengthens congregational singing. Encourage the choir members to help the congregation sing, not to perform themselves. The use of descants by choirs during hymns strengthens congregational singing. Make certain your song leader encourages congregational song. When your song leader brings out the talents of the people, the music is strengthened. Yet, when song leaders become performers, the people watch the leader, and the singing decreases. Song leaders are especially helpful in a cappella singing (which may be used for a whole hymn or just one stanza of a hymn).

Congregational singing can be strengthened in many different ways. You can preach sermons based on hymns; use hymns as prayers; sponsor hymn festivals; encourage antiphonal (responsive) singing of hymns in various combinations (for example, men alternating with women, left side alternating with right side, and choir alternating with the congregation); dramatize the words of a hymn; make a banner for a hymn; use familiar words with new tunes; use new words with familiar tunes; use "concertatos" (anthem settings of familiar hymns where the choir sings the more difficult parts and the congregation joins in on a part of the anthem); encourage hymn memorization; let the children teach new hymns to the congregation; sponsor a hymn-writing contest; lead a hymn class; write bulletin notes about hymns; or use a hymn as a theme of the day or season. See *The Hymns of The United Methodist Hymnal* for more suggestions.

## OPENING PRAYER(S)

*Almighty God,*
*to you all hearts are open, all desires known,*
*and from you no secrets are hidden.*
*Cleanse the thoughts of our hearts*
*by the inspiration of your Holy Spirit,*
*that we may perfectly love you,*

*and worthily magnify your holy name,
through Christ our Lord.
Amen.*

The opening prayers begin the dialogue between God and God's people. They set the tone of the day—celebration, confession, thanksgiving, and so forth. The tone can and should vary week by week. And the prayers must involve your whole congregation. They may be said in unison, responsively, or by a worship leader on behalf of all. The key to an effective opening prayer is its corporate, binding quality that focuses your congregation's attention.

An act of praise, such as a choir anthem, a children's song, a psalm reading, or a chorus may or may not follow the opening prayer(s).

## Proclamation and Response

*Lord, open our hearts and minds
by the power of your Holy Spirit,
that, as the scriptures are read
and your Word proclaimed,
we may hear with joy what you say to us today.
Amen.*

Recovering the pulpit is necessary if our denomination is to survive as a faithful witness to God. This emphasis comes to focus in Proclamation and Response. Proclamation and Response comprise the second major movement of worship, after Entrance, and the most important. In Proclamation and Response, the Word of God is read, proclaimed, and responded to.

Proclamation and Response comprise the most important element in the worship service, and thus it requires more time, effort, skills, and resources than any other part of worship.

### SCRIPTURE

On the Day of Pentecost at Royal Oaks United Methodist Church, Kathy, a high school junior, read the lesson from Acts in Spanish. We thought no one in the congregation understood Spanish. Some people looked bewildered, while others listened intently. Following the service, an older member approached Kathy with tears. This woman had been raised in

Puerto Rico, but had left her home many years before. She now spoke English, not Spanish. But on that day, for the first time in decades, she heard the scripture read in her native language.

The scripture is part of God's Word for us, and a goal of worship and evangelism is for your congregation to be biblically literate. There is a deep longing among all people for worship that proclaims God's Word.

Becoming more biblical in your worship services requires much effort. Pew Bibles or lesson inserts should be available. Encourage your members to bring Bibles to church. (To promote continuity, you may wish to encourage everyone to use one translation.) A pulpit Bible should be visible, and your readers should read from it. Practice reading the Bible clearly, distinctly, and audibly. Encourage laypersons to read the lessons in worship. Develop readers' abilities to read the scripture with feeling so that the spoken Word conveys both power and meaning. Help can be found in *Reading Scripture Aloud* by Richard Ward.

Tell people a week in advance what Bible passages will be used the following week. Begin a Wednesday evening or Thursday morning Bible study to help laity and clergy prepare together for preaching. Use language that is inclusive. The biblical witness, especially as it has been translated over the past several centuries, has excluded women and children. If you wish to include more people in worship, your reading of scripture must not exclude them.

Reading the scripture begins an active dialogue or conversation between the Word and your people. As each lesson is read, your congregation must then respond to it. Historically the Psalms have been responses to the Old Testament lessons. A hymn may be a response to the lessons of the Old and New Testaments. And the sermon is clearly a response to the lessons and a call for further response on the part of the people.

## **SERMON**

> Come, divine Interpreter,
> bring me eyes thy book to read,
> ears the mystic words to hear,
> words which from thee proceed,
> words that endless bliss impart,
> kept in an obedient heart.
> Charles Wesley, *Come, Divine Interpreter*

At Altamont United Methodist Church, a few people gathered on a snowy night. The yearly revival was under way, but the sudden snowstorm had kept many people away. Yet, the Bible was read and the Word proclaimed. Junior heard the Word for him, and he came forward.

The goal of a sermon is "to preach Jesus Christ in a way that allows the people to hear God's word for them and that invites corporate and personal responses" (Morris, pp. 58 ff.). Remember, John Wesley had an Arminian theology, which emphasized personal accountability for responding to God. And as a black United Methodist pastor in Jamaica, New York, declared, every sermon ought "to challenge people."

The content of a sermon should be the gospel story. Preachers must share the gospel out of faith and encourage gospel sharing by helping people get the story straight, from creation to the redemption of all the world.

Sermon preparation should be done carefully. The preacher begins with his or her own devotional life. Scripture study, prayer, fasting, frequent Communion, and spiritual fellowship are all important. In addition, the preacher must know the spirit of the people. Through visitation and counseling, the pastor must overhear the hurts and hopes of the congregation.

Only after personal devotion and attentiveness to the congregation can the pastor begin sermon preparation. Begin preparing sermons at least a season in advance. Make a file folder for each sermon. Look briefly at the lessons and catch the tone and thrust of the scripture for each service. Begin doing exegesis and personal reflection. Study with peers and with the congregation. The goal is to be grasped by the scripture so that it can be proclaimed with integrity.

The style of the sermon must be authentic. Sermon styles vary, but each style should exhibit a few common elements. The style should be oral, and it should be relational. The sermon must engage the people and the preacher in a dialogue with each other and with God. The style should be narrative. Recent homiletical studies have greatly enriched and expanded the understanding of narrative theology and preaching. The goal of a sermon is not to tell interesting stories, but to tell the gospel narrative in a way that draws persons of all ages, races, sexes, and conditions into that narrative. The task is complex, yet rewarding, when well done. For help, see *Preaching Pilgrims* by Michael Williams.

Finally, children's sermons or times must also be considered in their worship and evangelistic context. Do not relegate your children to a back room for children's church or ignore them in corporate worship. Children,

# Entrance and Proclamation

too, need God's converting, justifying, and sanctifying grace. And while the goal and content are the same as for all adult sermons, the methods must be radically different. Children do not understand object lessons. They need stories and times for sharing their faith. See "Proclaiming the Word with Children" in *God's Children in Worship* by Discipleship Resources.

In summary, as people enter your worship and hear the Word read and proclaimed, the dialogue between God and the people has begun. A call has been offered and some responses have been made. Now is the time to consider those responses in depth.

# 3. SERVICE OF WORSHIP: INVITATIONS AND RESPONSES

> Whether the Word be preached or read,
> no saving benefit I gain
> from empty sounds or letters dead;
> unprofitable all and vain,
> unless by faith thy Word I hear
> and see its heavenly character.
> Charles Wesley, "Whether the Word Be Preached or Read"

As a young pastor, Andy believed that invitations were inappropriate in worship. Rebelling against the "sawdust trail" style of evangelism, he was convinced that invitational worship appealed to the emotional side of the human character and thus was a partial and inadequate expression of the Christian faith. Only as he was taught and studied classical Wesleyan theology did he realize how wrong he was. For years he had proclaimed glorious visions of the kingdom of God, yet rarely had he offered people a passageway into God's realm.

Following the sermon, pastor Joe Pennel issued an invitation: "I offer an invitation to non-members here this morning. If God has spoken to you today, and, in response, if you wish to offer yourself in ministry and service with this congregation, I invite you to come forward and join this congregation." Stacy heard the call, came forward, and joined Belmont United Methodist Church.

When the Word of God has been read and proclaimed faithfully, responses are natural. The nature of invitations and responses is complex, but a few characteristics are universally present. First, invitations initiate responses. Invitations are catalysts of responses. Second, the variety of invitations and responses is great. For too long congregations have not recognized the variety of ways people can respond to the gospel.

## Invitations as Catalysts

The Avery Parish was becoming a community dedicated to mission work. Several persons had heard of the Volunteers in Mission program of The United Methodist Church. This program sent lay workers to foreign countries to live and work for two weeks at a time. In Panama, a Methodist parsonage and dormitory needed to be rebuilt. On a Sunday morning in October, following a sermon on mission, invitations were extended for volunteers. We expected four volunteers, but eight persons came forward. Now because too many people had responded, we were short of the funds needed to send the volunteers to Panama. For the next four weeks during the time of offering, the people were challenged to raise $6,000 (one-fifth of the year's total parish budget). In four weeks the people exceeded the challenge. Within two months the parish, in response to a gospel call, sent eight persons to Panama as witnesses of God's gracious activity.

An invitation is the "logical, sequential request" that comes from the Word of God proclaimed, yet the invitation does not presuppose a specific response (Martin, *Invite* p. 50). It is imperative, therefore, that your worship leaders ask and expect persons to answer the call of the gospel. Yet, what is the nature of this invitation?

First, invitations should be a regular part of your worship. Every service of worship should include an invitation and seek a response. As pastor Zan Holmes of Dallas once noted, too few pastors offer invitations and even fewer expect a response. As a New York district superintendent wrote, "Many pastors do not preach for a decision, nor do they call for one, nor do they witness many. This applies not only for decisions to accept and follow Jesus Christ as Lord and Savior, but also to make clear decisions about everything else."

Second, invitations should be specific, clear, and unambiguous. Invitations should tell people what they are to say, see, do, or become. If an invitation needs to be explained, make that explanation prior to the sermon, such as, "Following the sermon today, I will invite you to. . . ." But remember, having been specific, you must relax and let the Holy Spirit do its work.

Examples of specific invitations are numerous. Invite:

- non-members to join the church,
- youth to help create a more just society,
- sinners to repent and believe,
- saints to go on to perfection,
- the sick to be healed,
- families to strengthen home life,
- the rich to give away their possessions,
- visitors to join the fellowship,

# Invitations and Responses

- spouses to forgive marital wrongs,
- children to experience God's love, and
- older adults to anticipate the kingdom.

Our congregations ought to offer invitations to children as well as to adults. Sally accepted an invitation to Christian discipleship and baptism at age nine. Bishop Paul Duffey was received into church membership at age eight. Numerous examples remind the church that children, no less than adults, are open to God's loving power. (For additional help in involving children in worship, see the intergenerational resource: *God's Children in Worship*.) Whenever the church begins to think that a relationship to Christ is limited to persons of a certain age, we must remember Jesus' admonition: "Let the little children come unto me" (Matthew 19:13-15).

Third, all invitations must be personal. During the camp meetings in the early nineteenth century, exhorters were a special class of worship leaders. Always laypeople, they followed the sermons of the preaching clergy and made the word explicit and personal: "Brother Jones, you have been unfaithful to your wife!" "Sister Manfield, you have not attended your class meeting!" Today, we need worship leaders to act like exhorters who offer oral (not written and read!) invitations addressed to individuals and whole congregations, and who make the prophetic dimensions of preaching clear and unmistakable. Or, as Sallie Wiseman, a member of Pisgah United Methodist Church, remarked, "I want you to step on my toes."

Fourth, invitations should call for a deeper relationship with the Lord. The final goal is not a satisfying emotional experience or a provocative stimulus to further thought. Rather, the goal is to help persons be open to their deepest needs for God's grace.

## The Variety of Invitations and Responses

"Come to the altar and pray."
"Repent and believe the Gospel."
"I invite you to the feast of our Lord."

While all invitations should be regular, specific, personal, and should bring about a deeper relationship with God, invitations and responses must be varied. While every pastor or worship leader will have a more regular style of invitation, such as time for silent prayer or altar prayer time, it is important that invitations not become ordinary. There are at least nine major types of invitations and responses: biblical invitations; altar calls; occasions for silent prayer; invitations for vocal responses; invitations for other active responses; invitations to church membership; invitations to healing; confession, pardon, and peace; and the offering. Your worship leaders should include this whole range of invitations in the worship life of your congregation.

## BIBLICAL INVITATIONS AND RESPONSES

The biblical invitations and responses are fascinating because of their richness and unpredictability. Most reflect God's unconditional grace, yet each is contingent upon human receptivity. Here are just a few examples:

- "Be faithful and multiply, and fill the earth and subdue it; and have dominion . . ." (Genesis 1:28a).
- "Go in, tell Pharaoh king of Egypt to let the people of Israel go out of his land" (Exodus 6:11).
- "Return, O Israel, to the LORD your God" (Hosea 14:1).
- "Go, prophesy to my people Israel" (Amos 7:15).
- "Follow me" (Matthew 4:19).
- "Pray then like this . . ." (Matthew 6:9 ff).
- "Take, eat, this is my body" (Matthew 26:26).
- "Love your enemies" (Matthew 5:44).
- "Come to me, all who labor and are heavy laden" (Matthew 11:28).
- "Let not your hearts be troubled" (John 14:17).
- "If you want to come after me, you must deny yourself and take up your cross and follow me" (Matthew 16:24).
- "Go, therefore, and make disciples of all nations" (Matthew 28:19).
- "Repent and believe in the gospel" (Mark 1:15).
- "Take up your pallet and go home" (Mark 2:11).
- "This is my commandment, that you love one another as I have loved you" (John 15:12).
- "Repent and be baptized" (Acts 2:38).
- "Present your bodies as a living sacrifice, holy and acceptable to God" (Romans 12:1).

This listing is just a sampling of biblical invitations. It is difficult not to find an invitation in almost every biblical narrative.

# Invitations and Responses

And the responses were overwhelming!: the earth populated, a people liberated, the law created, a nation chastised, a prophecy proclaimed, a kingdom redeemed, love revealed, new life received, discipleship begun, prayer offered, forgiveness offered and received, persons baptized, a holy meal celebrated, sick persons healed, sinners redeemed, and a church created. All these responses and more came after biblical invitations.

Although the variety is great, the invitations and responses in these texts have much in common. First, the responses called for were appropriate to both the setting and the people. Jesus told sinners to go and sin no more. Also, the invitations were not predictable, in that they often did not fit traditional expectations. Who would have expected God to call Moses to speak to Pharaoh?

Each week, as the scripture is read and studied for worship, look for the invitations, explicit or implicit, in the texts. Use those invitations on that day, and expect responses.

## ALTAR CALLS

Terry Duckworth, a pastor in North Carolina, and William K. Quick in Detroit, typically conclude each service of worship with an altar call. At times no one comes, yet, on occasion, someone does. They persist because they are convinced that it is important.

Altar calls are valuable invitations, particularly for individuals within your congregation. They are markers in spiritual pilgrimage and public witnesses to personal commitment. They may be accompanied by a hymn, anthem, or instrumental music (hymns to be sung may include: "Come, Sinners, to the Gospel Feast" by Charles Wesley and all the hymns listed under "Invitation to Prayer" (951), "Invitation" (337-350), and "Repentance" (351-360) in *The United Methodist Hymnal*). Invite persons to come forward and either stand or kneel. At the altar, individuals or your whole congregation may offer private prayer, engage with another in prayer, make a public commitment, seek a healing touch, or make recommitments to Christ. The strength of an altar call, when it is open and hospitable, is the encouragement it gives persons to make a visible testimony before the community and to receive grace and support in return.

And when persons do come forward, your pastor and other worship leaders must support, endorse, and enable those who come. Kneel or stand with those who come. Pray, hug, touch, speak, offer words of grace, or speak words of pardon. In prayer, offer to persons God's presence by using the name of God. And always, the leader should tell those who respond that the pastor and others will be in touch and remain available throughout the days ahead.

When persons come forward to pray, the leaders should be ready to pray with them. According to Jim Wagner, the Director of the Upper Room Prayer Ministry, "The leader's role in praying with people is to be a channel, conduit, catalyst, compassionate friend, and an instrument of God's healing love." When you pray with others, let God do the work! The goal is to cooperate with God's desire and intention for wholeness. Therefore, leaders should concentrate on the loving, healing, forgiving presence of God by focusing on the problem solver rather than the problem and by focusing on wellness and wholeness rather than on sickness and sin. When persons come and ask for prayer:

- *Listen*. Ask each one who comes, "What is your prayer concern today?" and
- *Pray*. Briefly, quietly, and privately, lift up each person (and not the details) to God in the way that is natural and comfortable to you.

The time of prayer may be concluded with a hymn such as "Standing in the Need of Prayer" (352) or "Pass Me Not, O Gentle Savior" (351).

## OCCASIONS FOR SILENT PRAYER

The Sunday evening service at Lake Junaluska Assembly concluded with an invitation to prayer. Reginald Ponder, at the end of his sermon, asked that we put our hands on the seat in front of us, bend our foreheads to our hands, close our eyes, and pray to God. The silence was rich and deep. And our prayers rose like incense during that evening sacrifice.

Prayer time, for individuals and your whole congregation, requires invitation and response. With a background anthem or instrumental music, invite persons to stand, kneel, or sit in a devotional posture. Invite persons to offer prayers of commitment, petition, praise, reconciliation, intercession, and healing.

As persons are invited to pray, worship leaders must encourage that prayer by their actions. If you invite persons to kneel, kneel and let the people follow your actions. Be clear about what kinds of prayers are intended: intercession, thanksgiving, or some other kind. Give adequate time for prayer. While at first fifteen seconds may seem like a long period, over time three to five minutes may seem too short. And close with an appropriate prayer. For example: "Lord, having confessed our sins, we are a forgiven people. Thanks be to you!"

## INVITATIONS FOR VOCAL RESPONSES

At Louisa United Methodist Church, a small mountain congregation established by Francis Asbury, the Wednesday evening worship service moved toward its climax. Following the sermon, several members of the congregation stood at their seats and testified to what God had done that week. Included were personal testimonies of triumph over sin and a word of thanksgiving that an international confrontation had ended without bloodshed. The heritage of Asbury survived.

Invitations for vocal responses have been a part of the United Methodist tradition since the beginning. The Wesleys, Otterbein, and Boehm encouraged persons at worship to speak up about the mighty acts of God. Invite individuals within your community to clap their hands, to say "Amen," "Hallelujah," "Yes, Lord," or "Thank you, Jesus," or to select a hymn to sing. Invite your whole congregation to recite a creed, sing a hymn, or pray a collect or other unison prayer.

Several particular kinds of spoken responses are useful in all United Methodist congregations. One response is spontaneous, corporate prayer. In some congregations pastors enable the whole congregation to pray by encouraging the people themselves to say their own prayers out loud. These prayers are then responded to by the leader and people. For example, when a prayer is offered, the leader responds, "Lord, in your mercy," and the congregation then responds, "Hear our prayer." A pattern found in many Korean United Methodist churches is for the entire congregation to pray aloud simultaneously.

Another kind of spoken response is a prayer request. At Bethany United Methodist Church, the pastor receives prayer requests by moving along the center aisle of the sanctuary and asking persons to speak their prayers aloud. As each one is offered, the pastor repeats it boldly for all to hear. Upon returning to the pulpit area, a choir member hands the pastor a slip of paper with each prayer request listed. Particular needs, without exception, are always then lifted up to God.

Another response is a testimony. Particularly at times of intense spiritual transformation, encourage persons to testify about God in their own lives. These times might include the occasion when a person joins your congregation, when a person returns to worship after a time of grief, or when a person has renewed a commitment to God and the church. Help people in your congregations learn how to share publicly the ways God has offered them grace.

When requesting such responses, however, worship leaders must be prepared to respond. Tell the musician ahead of time that hymn requests will be received. Practice saying one of the creeds of the church. Move down out of the pulpit area to receive prayer requests or guide in corporate prayer. And gracefully respond when persons offer their testimonies. The whole movement of worship to include vocal responses to the invitation of the gospel is a dramatic sign that worship is the work of your people.

## INVITATIONS FOR OTHER ACTIVE RESPONSES

Following the scripture read and proclaimed, Jaquie Walker-Mishoe mimed a response to the Word—a person lifting up her heart to God. Her dramatic offering of the gospel embodied the congregation's need for sacrificial living.

Active responses to the gospel remind persons that they are not disembodied minds, hearts, mouths, and ears. Help persons offer their whole selves to God. Invite your congregation to stand, kneel, lift their hands to God, bow their heads, sway to the music, dance, mime, or clown their responses to the gospel. In a camp meeting, the pastor invited anyone who needed to ask forgiveness of any other member of the congregation to go to that person and ask. And for ten minutes, everyone did. Throughout all such responses, leaders must lead and guide the congregation. For example, if dance is offered, either participate or sit and give full attention. If you encourage people to kneel, show them how by doing it first. Unite the people by asking them to hold hands, form a circle, or hug or touch one another. Hymns such as "Amazing Grace" (378) and "Blessed Assurance" (369), as well as gospel choruses, are excellent hymns to sing on such occasions because so many know the words by heart.

Active responses might also include the calling forth of groups for ministry. A congregation in Decatur, Georgia offers worshipers the opportunity each Sunday to issue to others a call for a particular task or mission. If persons respond, the ministry proceeds; if no one responds, that means that the Holy Spirit is not moving in that direction. For example, one Sunday two young men called forth a group to start a magazine dealing with the Christian response to world hunger. As a result, the fine periodical *Seeds* had its beginning.

At Belmont United Methodist Church in Nashville, David Watson issued a call for persons to join Covenant Discipleship groups, and 125 persons came forward. People want to respond to the Word of God in ways that involve them in active ministry in the world.

## INVITATIONS TO CHURCH MEMBERSHIP*

How to

Join

[Your Church]
United Methodist Church

[Your Location]
[Your Address]
[Your City]
[Your Phone]

*Pages 32 through 35 comprise a brochure you may put in your pew rack.

Invitations and Responses

If you live in our community, we would welcome you into t[he mem]bership of [*Our Church*] United Methodist Church. You may join [in] several ways:

* * * * *

BY PROFESSION OF FAITH AND BAPTISM

If you are not now a baptized Christian, our pastor will be happy to discuss the meaning of baptism with you in your home or at the church at your convenience.

* * * * *

BY TRANSFER FROM ANOTHER UNITED METHODIST CHURCH

At your request, our pastor will get in touch with you. You do not need to write your former church. Our church will handle the details of transfer for you. You will be asked to take this vow at Sunday worship: "As a member of this congregation, will you faithfully participate in its ministries by your prayers, your presence, your gifts, and your service?"

* * * * *

BY TRANSFER FROM ANOTHER CHRISTIAN DENOMINATION

At your request, [*Our Church*] will write for your letter of membership at your former church. Since you have already been baptized, this step will not be repeated.

You will be asked to take the vows taken by all members of The United Methodist Church: "As a member of Christ's universal church, will you be loyal to The United Methodist Church, and do all in your power to strengthen its ministries?"
and
"As a member of this congregation, will you faithfully participate in its ministries by your prayers, your presence, your gifts, and your service?"

* * * * *

# Invitations and Responses

I wish to become a part of [*Our Church*] United Methodist Church.

( ) I want to confess my faith in Jesus Christ. I (have) (have not) been baptized.
( ) I want to transfer from the _____ United Methodist Church in _____.
( ) I want to transfer from the _____ Church in _____.
( ) I want to become an Affiliate Member. I will keep my membership at _____ United Methodist Church in _____.
( ) I want to become an Associate Member. I will keep my membership at _____ Church in _____.

Name: _____

Address: _____

Phone: _____

A classic invitation and response within our tradition is to join The United Methodist Church and a particular congregation. The invitation is offered to all persons who do not belong to a church. The most appropriate place for the invitation to membership follows the Word of God read and proclaimed. The invitation should be personal, oral, and specific. The sample brochure above defines clearly the steps for membership within our denomination. Such a document can help persons decide how and when to join. Place your own brochure in the pew racks in your sanctuary.

When persons join by profession of faith and baptism, the official ritual is "The Baptismal Covenant," which follows the Word read and proclaimed. In this rite God forgives sins, makes new creatures, makes children of God, incorporates persons into the church, and makes persons heirs of Christ. [See *Companion to the Book of Services* (Abingdon, 1988) by Hoyt Hickman and *The Worship Resources of The United Methodist Hymnal* (Abingdon 1989) by Hoyt Hickman for practical help on how to use "The Baptismal Covenant."]

At each full service of baptism, the pastor can invite persons to reaffirm their baptismal vows with symbolic use of water. These acts may include sprinkling water toward (not on) the people, lifting the water for all to see, lifting the baptismal bowl, or encouraging persons to come forward to touch the water, to place the water on their foreheads with the sign of the cross, or to wash their hands, face, or head.

When persons join by transfer from another United Methodist congregation, the official rite is found in "The Baptismal Covenant":

> "As a member of this congregation,
> will you faithfully participate in its ministries
> by your prayers, your presence,
> your gifts, and service?
> *I will.*"

When persons join by transfer from another Christian denomination, "The Baptismal Covenant" asks:

> "As a member of Christ's universal church,
> will you be loyal to The United Methodist Church,
> and do all in your power to strengthen its ministries?
> *I will.*"

and

> "As a member of this congregation,
> will you faithfully participate in its ministries
> by your prayers, your presence,
> your gifts, and your service?
> *I will.*"

# Invitations and Responses

When persons wish to become affiliate members or associate members of the congregation, there is no official service. Yet they should be invited forward, introduced, and welcomed as members of your congregation.

However persons decide to join, your congregation must encourage them to come and make their intention known publicly. As stated before, your corporate worship should help persons share publicly how God has offered them grace.

Finally, the congregation should welcome the new members at this time. The words of welcome and commendation in "The Baptismal Covenant I" (38) can be used:

*We give thanks for all that God has already given you
and welcome you in Christian love.
As members together with you
in the body of Christ
and in this congregation
of The United Methodist Church,
we renew our covenant
faithfully to participate
in the ministries of the church
by our prayers, our presence,
our gifts, and our service,
that in everything God may be glorified
through Jesus Christ.*

And more might also be done. In a black congregation in New York, the pastor invited the congregation to come welcome a new member. As the choir sang "Bless Be the Tie That Binds," the congregation greeted her warmly. Or, fellowship friends or sponsors could be named to stand with the new members. Such fellowship friends should be carefully chosen and encouraged to incorporate the new member into the life of the community. An excellent help for this ministry of incorporation is Suzanne Braden's *The First Year: Incorporating New Members into the Congregation.*

## INVITATION TO HEALING

At a retreat on Spiritual Formation for the Louisville, Kentucky, and Red Bird Conferences, Jim Wagner issued an invitation for persons to come forward and meet with a two-person team for prayer and anointing with oil for healing. Out of 250 persons present, some 50 individuals responded. In the name of God, persons offered and received prayer and anointing for healing.

A significant ministry is available for churches that offer services of healing. Remembering the healing ministry of Jesus, your congregation may help persons experience spiritual and physical reunion with God through Jesus Christ, receive healing and forgiveness in their relationships with God and others, renew their trust in God's love and mercy for all people, and find hope in the midst of darkness and despair.

The essential elements of such an invitation and response are:

- An open invitation to persons to come. The kinds of healing may need to be listed: of spirit, mind, body, and relationships.
- A time to listen to persons as they share their concerns and needs.
- An anointing, with or without oil (a pure oil such as olive oil), using the thumb or forefinger, while making the sign of the cross on the forehead.
- A brief, private prayer to God for the person, such as:
"Lord Jesus, strengthen and heal this child. May your healing love and power flow into her life. Banish all pain, sickness, and sin. Give her your blessings of health in body, mind, spirit, and relationships. We ask these things in the name of the Father, Son, and Holy Spirit. Amen."

During this service, the following hymns may be sung:

- "Heal Me, Hands of Jesus" (262)
- "Heal Us, Emmanuel, Hear Our Prayer" (266)
- "O Christ, the Healer" (265)
- Other Hymns of healing (943).

An intentional and holistic ministry of healing may become one of the most exciting ministries of your church in worship and evangelism. For further information, read Jim Wagner's *Blessed to Be a Blessing*.

## CONFESSION, PARDON, AND PEACE

Christ our Lord calls all who love him
earnestly to repent of their sin
and live in peace with one another.
Therefore, let us confess our sin before God and one another.
*Merciful God,*
*we confess that we have not loved you with our whole heart.*
*We have failed to be an obedient church.*

# Invitations and Responses

*We have not done your will,*
*we have broken your law,*
*we have rebelled against your love,*
*we have not loved our neighbors,*
*and we have not heard the cry of the needy.*
*Forgive us, we pray.*
*Free us for joyful obedience,*
*through Jesus Christ our Lord.*
*Amen.*
Hear the good news:
   Christ died for us while we were yet sinners;
   that proves God's love toward us.
In the name of Jesus Christ, you are forgiven!
*In the name of Jesus Christ, you are forgiven!*
*Glory to God. Amen.*

Tom Langford was uncomfortable passing the peace. Yet in the seminary chapel he stood, shook hands with his neighbors, and was hugged by an older woman student. Although he didn't like to be hugged in a public forum, he yielded while grumbling to himself. Following the service, the woman spoke to him as they left: "As a divorced woman with no children, the passing of the peace is a highlight. It is the only time during the week when I touch another person." Tom was humbled by her remark.

Confession, pardon, and peace form an integrated whole in an effective worship service. The call to confession invites persons to recognize their alienation from God. Prayers of confession, in response, may be unison prayers, pastoral prayers, silent prayers, or bidding prayers. The latter are more effective in letting persons be in immediate dialogue with God. On occasion, because your whole congregation or community may need to seek God's pardoning grace, a whole service of reconciliation may be appropriate.

In response to prayers of confession, words of pardon declare God's good news of forgiveness. Worship leaders may speak these words forcefully or gently; the goal is to help persons appropriate Jesus' words: "Your sins are forgiven." Do not underestimate the need of persons to hear this good news. And the passing of the peace is a public demonstration by your people, forgiven and reconciled by God, of their forgiveness of and reconciliation with their neighbors. The peace should not be a polite time of shaking hands with friends and exchanging superficial information, but a physical embodiment of grace. Let people stand and touch, hug, or kiss one another. And worship leaders must take the lead in passing the peace. If the leader is comfortable and relaxed, and responds joyfully to this opportunity, so will the congregation.

## OFFERING

*As forgiven and reconciled people,*
*let us offer ourselves and our gifts to God.*

Andy's and Sally's grandmothers occasionally took them to church when they were children. A vivid memory for both is that when the pastor issued the call for the giving of tithes and offerings, the grandmothers quietly placed a coin in their hands. The children then placed the coin carefully in the offering plate. Not knowing (but maybe knowing), their grandmothers taught Andy and Sally Christian stewardship.

The offering is the vital and necessary link between the Word of God and the Table of our Lord. More than the raising of funds, the offering should be a model of Christian stewardship: As God has given to us, we now give back to God. And your offerings should call for more than your financial gifts. Gifts should include the time and talents God has given.

An Atlanta congregation recruits Sunday school teachers during the offering. A Dallas congregation receives a dance during the offering. A New York congregation promotes voter registration during the offering. A South Carolina church receives the gifts of bread and cup from a young family. All of these are examples of how the offering may be a time of invitation. Methods include distributing and receiving a talent card, passing around worksheets, or soliciting volunteers for church work. Invite and receive a multiplicity of gifts.

The gifts should also include the sacrificial offering of the material wealth of your congregation. Some of our Black United Methodist congregations receive multiple offerings during worship. Often congregations receive too little because they expect too little. And the style of receiving makes a difference. While, typically, many United Methodist congregations pass offering plates, on occasion persons should be asked to come forward and place their gifts on the altar or table.

Encourage everyone to participate in the time of offering. In our increasingly "cashless society," people are too often only occasionally (biweekly or monthly) responding to the offering, or they do so only by mail. This practice promotes a relationship with God that makes the offering a business transaction. Encourage every person to make an offering of some kind every week. The response may be one dollar or a talent card, yet such gifts show active responses to God's grace. And music, especially as sung by the whole congregation, adds greatly to the offering. In addition to the traditional doxology, sing "All Things Come of Thee" (588) and "Bless Thou the Gifts" (587). And include everyone in the offering. Children and youth are often passed over. Give them the opportunity to respond. One Virginia congregation encourages children to write on a blank 3" × 5" card one thing that they will do for God in the coming week and to place their offering in the plate. This may also be an excellent model for adults to follow.

# 4. SERVICE OF WORSHIP: THANKSGIVING WITH COMMUNION AND SENDING FORTH

The previous discussion of invitations and responses arises particularly out of the Protestant worship tradition over the past several hundred years. Yet such styles of invitations and responses stand within a broader and richer tradition of call and response. Today, in The United Methodist Church, we need to recover the fundamental invitations and responses of the historic and universal church: The Baptismal Covenant and Holy Communion or the Lord's Supper.

As Charles Wesley wrote:
> Come let us use the grace divine,
> and all with one accord,
> in a perpetual covenant join
> ourselves to Christ the Lord;
> give up ourselves, thru Jesus' power,
> his name to glorify;
> and promise, in this sacred hour,
> for God to live and die.
>
> "Come Let Us Use the Grace Divine"

## The Baptismal Covenant

A young couple brings their infant child to the service for baptism. A young person makes a personal confession of Christ as Savior in a service of confirmation. A young woman recommits herself in a service of baptismal reaffirmation. And a whole Annual Conference reaffirms the Baptismal Covenant. All of these are visible signs of hearing and responding to God's Word.

The Baptismal Covenant—Holy Baptism, Confirmation, Reaffirmation of Faith, Reception into The United Methodist Church, and Reception into a Congregation—testifies to a central reality of God's grace that has claimed persons and a community. The introduction to the service, found in *The Book of Services* (approved by the 1984 General Conference and included in *The United Methodist Hymnal*), states:

Through the Sacrament of baptism,
we are initiated into Christ's holy church.
We are incorporated into God's mighty acts of salvation
and given new birth through water and the Spirit.
All this is God's gift, offered to us without price.

In this covenant, persons and congregations renounce the spiritual forces of wickedness, accept the freedom and power God gives, confess Jesus Christ as Savior, commit themselves to the church, profess the Christian faith, and are saved through water and the Spirit.

Such services most properly follow the sermon as a response to the Word read and proclaimed. And such services must be planned and led well. Preparation should include time with the persons and families involved in a baptism. Congregations should be trained and taught well the meaning of the sacrament. Resources such as William Willimon's *Remember Who You Are* or Hoyt Hickman's *A Primer for Church Worship* are excellent teaching books.

The liturgical leadership of The Baptismal Covenant demands particular attention by the pastor. Clergy should review Hoyt Hickman's *Companion to The Book of Services* and *The Worship Resources of The United Methodist Hymnal*. Here are some other suggestions to enrich your practice of baptism:

- Baptize particularly on the days of the Baptism of the Lord, Easter, Pentecost, and All Saints'.
- Nonverbally walk through the whole service to be sure that every action corresponds to the text spoken.
- Baptize before the whole congregation at the regular worship service.
- Keep the baptismal font or pool continually in view. This should also be done on Sundays without baptisms.
- Let the water be visible: Pour the water from a clear glass pitcher into the font or pool.
- Thoroughly wet the candidate by dipping infants or using immersion or pouring.
- Enable the congregation to watch the whole action. Ask parents, sponsors, and family members to stand to the side of the pastor.
- Seal the candidate with oil, using a pure oil and marking the candidate's forehead, mouth, and heart with the sign of the cross.
- Put new clothes on the initiate. A baptismal bib, gown, or stole may be made by the congregation.
- Light a Christ candle.

Never underestimate the power of the sign action of a baptism to demonstrate the basic dynamic of call and response. When an infant or a child is baptized, the congregation remembers God's love. When a young person makes the first public reaffirmation of faith (confirmation), the people remember that responses are required. And when an adult yields to God's summons and is baptized, the congregation recalls that God's grace works in mysterious and powerful ways.

The following hymns in *The United Methodist Hymnal* will add to the service of the Baptismal Covenant:

- "Child of Blessing, Child of Promise" (611) for the baptism of a child
- "Come, Let Us Use the Grace Divine" (606), a classic Wesley text
- "Praise and Thanksgiving Be to God" (604) for a Service of Reaffirmation
- "This Is the Spirit's Entry Now" (608) to be sung during the Thanksgiving over the water
- "You Have Put on Christ" (609) to be sung by a whole congregation following the Baptismal Covenant

In this context, the Service of a Congregational Reaffirmation of the Baptismal Covenant (Baptismal Covenant IV(50)) is one of the most powerful worship and evangelistic experiences. In this service, used only when no persons are to be baptized, confirmed, or received into the church, the whole congregation renounces Satan, accepts freedom, confesses Christ, and affirms the faith. Then with liturgical acts that are not mistaken for baptism (such as the water being lifted for all to see, water being sprinkled toward the people, or persons coming forward to touch the water or to touch the water to their head, face, or heart), the people remember that they have been baptized and are thankful. This service, as experienced with eight hundred clergy in the Western North Carolina Conference, caused one retired pastor to say to Bishop L. Bevel Jones, "This was the most evangelistic service we have ever had in this Conference."

## The Lord's Supper

For John Wesley, the Lord's Supper was the archetypal response by Christians to the grace God reveals to us in Jesus Christ. It could be a converting sacrament for persons who did not believe, a justifying sacrament for those who needed God's love, and a sanctifying sacrament for the saints going on to perfection.

> Come, sinners, to the gospel feast,
> let every soul be Jesus' guest.
> You need not one be left behind,
> for God hath bid all humankind.
> Charles Wesley, "Come, Sinners, to the Gospel Feast"

As with The Baptismal Covenant, the service of Holy Communion properly follows a full sermon as a response to the Word read and proclaimed. Not to preach (or to offer a mini-sermon) denies the connection between call and response and assumes response without a call.

Preparation should include spending time with persons in the community. The American Wesleyan tradition of open communion often evolves into lax discipline. Instead of invitations to love Christ, repent of sins, and live in peace, invitations too often sound like a game show invitation, "Come on down." The invitation should be to all baptized Christians, of whatever age or tradition, and to unbaptized persons who intend to become a part of the Body of Christ. The invitation to eat and drink with Christ demands serious consideration by every individual present and, at times, strong pastoral intervention. Congregations should study William Willimon's *Sunday Dinner* and Hoyt Hickman's *A Primer for Church Worship*. Invitations ought to be clear so that responses are authentic.

The liturgical leadership of Holy Communion also demands serious attention by the pastor. Clergy should review the relevant chapters of Hickman's *Companion to the Book of Services* and *The Worship Resources of The United Methodist Hymnal*. Other suggestions to enrich your practice of the Lord's Supper include:

- Serve more frequently: weekly or monthly. Especially celebrate in relation to the Christian year: the first Sunday of Advent, Christmas Eve or Day, the Day of Epiphany, the first Sunday of Lent, Passion/Palm Sunday, Holy Thursday, Easter Vigil, Day of Easter, Day of Pentecost, and All Saints' Day.
- Vary the worship settings: sanctuary, fellowship hall, garden, homes, or camp settings.
- Center the worship space on the altar or table.
- Pull the altar or table away from a back wall or pulpit and use a free-standing, rectangular table.
- Clear the visual barriers between the altar or table and people.
- Clear the table of all clutter.

# Thanksgiving with Communion and Sending Forth 47

- Paraments, stoles, and banners should be those of the Christian year (not exclusively white).
- Let all four actions of the Lord's Supper be visible: take, bless, break, and give. Specifically:

1. *Taking the Bread and Cup:*
   Use a whole loaf of bread and large cup (chalice).
   Encourage members of the congregation to make and prepare the elements.
   Bring in the elements with the offering of the day. Let those who prepare the elements offer them to the congregation.

2. *Prayer of Great Thanksgiving:*
   The pastor should stand behind the table, facing the people.
   Use the "orans" position for prayer (head erect or lifted, arms out at side and flexed, palms forward).
   Encourage the congregation to stand.
   Use the appropriate "Prayer of Great Thanksgiving" that blesses God for the gifts of creation and redemption, tells the meaning of our actions at the Lord's table, and invokes the power of the Holy Spirit.
   Practice *extempore* Prayers of Great Thanksgiving.
   See *Holy Communion* for various prayers.
   Sing the congregational responses to the prayer:
   the Sanctus and Benedictus, the Memorial Acclamation, and the Great Amen in *The United Methodist Hymnal* (17, 18, 20, 23, 24).
   Conclude with the Lord's Prayer. Sing the Lord's Prayer (270, 271, 894-896).

3. *Breaking the Bread:*
   The pastor lifts the bread and breaks it, with or without words. All should see the action.
   The pastor raises the cup, with or without words. All should see the action.

4. *Giving the Bread and Cup:*
   Invite all persons to the table, yet allow persons to abstain without embarrassment. Enable persons with handicapping conditions to receive at their seats.
   Let ushers be gentle guides, aiding the congregation to come to

the table. To aid members and visitors, explain how communion is to be received and who will be invited to receive, either in the bulletin or as an announcement before the service. Encourage children of all ages to receive.

Use baptized laypersons to distribute the elements.

Encourage people to receive bread by placing right hand on left palm, creating a small cross or a throne for the gift.

The giving of bread and cup is primarily nonverbal, but words may be used.

When serving, maintain good eye contact, speak the person's name, and touch a hand.

Avoid "self-service communion," which diminishes the communal quality of the meal and negates "giving and receiving."

## STYLES OF DISTRIBUTION

Communion services in Advent, Lent, and other times of penitence (such as revivals) demand a style of distribution that encourages people to kneel and be humble in the presence of God. Each of the following styles enables people to be more reflective as they receive and meditate upon the Lord's Supper. On these days, while the people move quietly during the distribution, the choir may sing anthems.

- Pastors and lay servers stand in front of the communion rail. People form a single line, come one by one to the servers, kneel (or stand), receive the elements, and then either proceed to the communion rail to kneel and pray, returning to their seats when they wish, or return immediately to their seats after receiving, for a time of prayer and meditation. This style of distribution takes the least amount of time of these three methods.
- Pastors and lay servers stand in pairs behind the Communion rail. Individuals, when they desire, come to the Communion rail and kneel. A pair of servers immediately provides the elements. Individuals may then remain for silent prayer as long as they wish and then return to their seats. When one person leaves the rail, another takes that place, and the pattern is repeated. This style requires a longer time for distribution.
- Pastors and servers stand behind the Communion rail. People come by tables (small groups) and kneel together; all receive the elements at the same time, hear a blessing, rise, and return to

# Thanksgiving with Communion and Sending Forth

their seats. Then another table comes forward. This style takes the longest time of any method of distribution.

Communion services at Christmas, Easter, and other joyful times (such as All Saints' Day) demand a style of distribution that encourages the mingling and free movement of people. Each of the following styles enables people to rejoice in the Lord's Supper, and in each style, the Lord's Supper is distributed in a relatively short time on these days. The whole congregation may sing hymns during the distribution.

- Pastors and servers stand at the table, divide the elements, and place them on trays. Servers then pass the trays from person to person, pew to pew, each person serving the one seated next to him or her. This method takes the least amount of time.
- Pastors and servers divide into pairs and stand at several places in the worship area. People then come, stand, and receive from the servers closest to them. People then return to their seats. This method takes a longer time.
- Pastors and servers stand at one place at the front of the sanctuary. People form a single line, come, stand, receive, and return to their seats. This method takes the most time of these three methods.

The use of music dramatically heightens the quality of the Lord's Supper. The leaders of worship might want to teach the congregation the full Communion service from the Anglican tradition (*Book of Hymns* #830 or Word and Table IV in *The United Methodist Hymnal*). Keep in mind that the mood of that service is more penitential and confessional than the services of Word and Table I, II, and III in the new hymnal.

Whether or not the congregation sings during the serving of the sacraments is a decision to be made by the pastor and the worship committee. If you do sing hymns, be sure to choose enough so that you do not run out of hymns before everyone receives. Choose hymns that match the tone of the sacrament—penitential hymns during Lent and joyful hymns on Easter and Pentecost. If you do sing, try these hymns in the large section of *The United Methodist Hymnal* entitled "Eucharist (Holy Communion or the Lord's Supper)" (see *The Hymns of The United Methodist Hymnal* for more information):

- "Here, O My Lord, I See Thee Face to Face" (623). Use first three

stanzas before or while receiving and stanzas four and five after receiving.
- "Take Our Bread" (640) and "I Come with Joy" (617). Sing as the sacraments are brought forward during the offering.
- "O the Depth of Love Divine" (627). Charles Wesley wrote many hymns for the Lord's Supper. Recover these from *The United Methodist Hymnal* and other sources of Wesley materials, such as the Wesley Works project.
- "Become to Us the Living Bread" (630). Sing during the service.
- "Now Let Us from This Table Rise" (634). Sing following Communion.

Set the table in order when all have been served. Clean the cup and pick up the crumbs.

The remaining elements may be set aside for later distribution to the sick or others unable to attend. Clergy and laity may participate in this ministry. Or the remaining elements may be wholly consumed by the pastor and others as a sign of respect for the elements. Or the remaining elements may be returned to the earth, a biblical gesture of worship (see 2 Samuel 23:16) and an ecological symbol today. Whatever you choose to do with the remaining elements should express our stewardship of God's gifts and our respect for the purpose which these elements have served.

Remember, the Lord's Supper is an offering by God to the community of faith. When rightly offered and received, it is a means of convicting, justifying, and sanctifying grace. After it is offered, the community can pray:

> *Eternal God, we give you thanks for this holy mystery*
> *in which you have given yourself to us.*
> *Grant that we may go into the world*
> *in the strength of your Spirit,*
> *to give ourselves for others,*
> *in the name of Jesus Christ our Lord.*
> *Amen.*

## Sending Forth

"Daddy King," the father of Dr. Martin Luther King, Jr., preached at Duke Chapel in 1978. At the conclusion of the service, he stood before the congregation, raised his hands, and, in a booming, rich voice, charged

# Thanksgiving with Communion and Sending Forth

the people to go forth and create a society of peace and justice. The people knew their commission.

The "sending forth," the final movement of worship, gathers together the whole service of worship and directs the people to spread God's grace throughout all creation. It is the link between Sunday and Monday and between the people at worship and the people at work. This is the time to invite persons to be witnesses for peace and justice in the world. Send the people forth, empowered by God, to offer God's universal grace. If your church is to share God's steadfast love with all people, its worship must charge the whole community with this task in the sending forth. Here is an example.

> Called by worship to your service,
> forth in your dear name we go
> to the child, the youth, the aged,
> love in living deeds to show;
> hope and health, good will and comfort,
> counsel, aid, and peace we give,
> that your servants, Lord, in freedom
> may your mercy know, and live.
> Albert Bayl, "Lord, Whose Love Through Humble Service"

The final hymn of worship should refocus the invitation of the day away from the congregation to the community beyond the sanctuary walls. Encourage the people to sing the hymn as if it were their call to ministry and mission. Hymns might include:

- "Go Forth for God" (670)
- "Go, Make of All Disciples" (571)
- "God of Grace and God of Glory" (577)
- "God of Love and God of Power" (578)
- "Heralds of Christ" (567)
- "You Are the Seed" (583)
- "Lead On, O King Eternal" (580)
- "Lord, You Give the Great Commission" (584)
- "The Church of Christ, in Every Age" (589)
- "We've a Story to Tell to the Nations" (569)

Also check *The United Methodist Hymnal* under "Social Concerns" (952), "Closing Hymns" (939), and "Sending Forth" (952).

## DISMISSAL WITH BLESSING

*Go forth in peace.*
*The grace of the Lord Jesus Christ,*
*and the love of God,*
*and the communion of the Holy Spirit*
*be with you all.*
*Amen.*

The dismissal with blessing is a blessing on the people and a charge to be faithful disciples. Standing before the congregation and facing the people, the pastor should help the community focus its attention on the world and its task of making disciples. It is inappropriate at this point to receive new members because this would encourage the congregation to focus in on itself. Rather, pointing the whole congregation, including those received following the sermon, to the community beyond the sanctuary walls means that all are commissioned to act.

Musical blessings and dismissals are highly effective ways of sending forth. Music might include:

- "Lord, Dismiss Us with Thy Blessing" (671)
- "Sent Forth by God's Blessing" (664)
- One of the choral "Amens " (897-904)

## GOING FORTH

An inner-city congregation in Washington, D.C., concludes every service of worship with a fellowship hour. In the fellowship hall, coffee, tea, juice, and small snacks are shared as persons gather, meet, and build community. This scene is repeated in many growing United Methodist congregations.

In going forth, worship must be in continuity with how the community acts when all have left the sanctuary. Your congregation should encourage persons to respond to God's grace even after worship has ended. Encourage the dialogue to continue in informal settings, and tell people about these opportunities in your bulletins and announcements. For example, invite members and visitors to join the pastor in food or drink after worship, in conversation later that day, in a dinner following worship, in a new-member class (scheduled regularly), or in a quiet setting such as a chapel or office with the pastor or trained laity. The Billy

# Thanksgiving with Communion and Sending Forth

Graham crusades are effective because names and addresses are taken and careful, persistent follow-up occurs.

Incorporation of members is the necessary final stage of worship and evangelism. Incorporation is not automatic, and the responsibility to achieve it rests on the entire community. Time, effort, money, and people are required in an ongoing process. Your goals should be to include new members of the church in the community by helping them establish friendships, share their spiritual gifts, join a fellowship group, participate in financial campaigns, identify with the body, and attend worship. The most helpful resource now available on incorporation is Suzanne Braden's *The First Year: Incorporating New Members into the Congregation*.

As you strengthen worship in your congregation, remember that the power of God will be with you. As Peter preached to the persons in Jerusalem on the Day of Pentecost:

> "Repent, and be baptized every one of you in the name of Jesus Christ for the forgiveness of your sins; and you shall receive the gift of the Holy Spirit." . . . So those who received his word were baptized, and there were added that day about three thousand souls (Acts 2:38,41).

# 5. THE CHRISTIAN YEAR

In the fourth century, during the years following the Christian conversion of the Roman Emperor Constantine, the church faced a major crisis. By the Emperor's decree, all citizens of Rome became Christian. The mass baptisms that followed his decree fundamentally changed the character of the church. From a small sect with serious believers, the church became a great organization with many halfway Christians. How would the church teach all these persons the way of life in Christ?

One major answer was the Christian year. The church took important celebrations of the life of Jesus Christ and combined them into a systematic and comprehensive biblical narrative for telling the gospel story. Beginning in the winter, the church told of the anticipation of the Messiah, his birth, and his baptism. As the year continued, the narrative told of Christ's preparations for Jerusalem, his teachings, his dramatic entry, his passion, death, and resurrection. Finally, the church told of Christ's presence with the disciples for forty days, climaxing on the Day of Pentecost. Having told this story, what did the church do the next year? The church repeated the story from the Bible. Over and over again the church told of God's mighty acts. And a culture was transformed and renewed.

Today, in the late twentieth century, the church is again faced with a major crisis. Many profess to believe the gospel, but too few know the biblical witness and fewer still know what it means for individuals and all creation. Many people are biblically illiterate, and our culture is Christian in name only. How can the church today transform persons and society? How do we encourage spiritual formation? If the church tells too much too quickly, both the details and the large picture become blurred. The Christian year offers one solution by expressing the faith and proclaiming the gospel in a strong narrative style: how all creation longs for the coming One; the birth of the Messiah; his ministry and teachings; the passion, death and resurrection; and the full coming of the Holy Spirit on God's chosen people. We must tell the Bible story because it is God's story, and because by the story's very nature lives can be formed in the faith and be transformed into the image of Christ.

At the heart of the Christian year are two great cycles: the primary Lent/Easter/Pentecost cycle and the secondary Advent/Christmas/

Epiphany cycle. Each is a unified time that tells one story. In each, persons prepare for a unique manifestation of God in Jesus Christ. Then, the good news of God in Christ is proclaimed and celebrated in a season of joy. Each cycle of anticipation, proclamation, and celebration may now become normative for all persons who wait on the Lord, receive God's grace, and respond with faith, joy, and hope. The journey of the community becomes the journey of each individual. As the story is told over and over again, persons are initiated in the paschal mystery of Jesus Christ.

Today, God calls the church to tell the whole mysterious narrative of God's love to women, children, and men. As the narrative unfolds, layers of existence are revealed. There will be conflict and resistance as the divine narrative exposes the principalities and powers of this world. God's time reflects values that often stand in opposition to the values of society. Yet there will be success, for in the story God in Christ lives and acts and forms persons in the image of the divine. By celebrating the seasons of the Christian year and its festivals, time is transformed. By telling God's story, our own story becomes explicit, and we are formed as Christians. [Many of the services and ideas expressed in this chapter may be enriched by using *The Handbook of the Christian Year*. Please refer to it for clear suggestions on how to plan around the Christian year.]

> For as the rain and snow come down from heaven, and return not thither but water the earth, making it bring forth and sprout, giving seed to the sower and bread to the eater; so shall my word that goes forth from my mouth; it shall not return to me empty, but it shall accomplish that which I purpose, and prosper in the thing for which I sent it.
>
> Isaiah 55:10,11

## Advent/Christmas/Epiphany

At Pisgah United Methodist Church, the days of December witnessed a dramatic rise in activity. On the First Sunday of Advent, a Christmas tree appeared in the sanctuary. The children placed an Advent wreath on the flower table. Throughout the weeks ahead, women began baking for Christmas parties. The children's teachers organized their classes for the Christmas play, while the men began work on the set. The youth sang at the local rest home. On Christmas Eve, the annual pageant took place, complete with crying babies and many persons who came to church only for this occasion. The next morning, Christmas Day, the congregation celebrated the Lord's Supper, accompanied by the singing of Christmas

# The Christian Year

carols. And on the Sunday of Epiphany, the congregation renewed its baptismal covenant with God.

The events at Pisgah are typical of many congregations. The activities, centered around the Incarnation, call many persons and communities back to a renewed relationship with God. In this great cycle of Advent/Christmas/Epiphany, God responds to the need and longing of all creation for the Advent of the Messiah. God's response is the birth of a child who becomes a light to all the nations. In a single story of anticipation, birth, and manifestation, God's greatest gift offers spiritual renewal to a people who sit in darkness.

## **ADVENT**

There was a time when John the Baptist appeared, preaching in the desert of Judea and saying, "Repent, for the kingdom of God is at hand."

John's clothes were made of camel's hair, and he had a leather belt around his waist. Grasshoppers and wild honey were his food. From Jerusalem and all Judea and the whole region of the Jordan, people were going out to John. Confessing their sins, they were baptized by him in the Jordan River.

But when John saw many of the Pharisees and Sadducees coming to where he was baptizing, he said to them: "You brood of vipers! Who warned you to flee from the coming wrath? Give some evidence that you mean to repent. And do not think you can tell yourselves, 'We have Abraham [and Sarah] as our ancestors.' I tell you that out of these stones God can raise up descendants for Abraham [and Sarah]. The axe is already at the root of the trees, and every tree that is not fruitful will be cut down and thrown into the fire."

[And John said:] "I baptize you with water, for repentance. But after me will come one who is more powerful than I am, whose sandals I am not fit to carry. He will baptize you with the Holy Spirit and with fire. With winnowing fork in hand, he will clear his threshing floor, gathering the wheat into his barn and burning up the chaft with a fire that will never go out."

Matthew 3;1-2,4-12<br>Second Sunday of Advent<br>Year A

Each year, the season of Advent follows a pattern that encourages an appraisal of the need for Jesus Christ. Each year, this pattern occurs:

- The first Sunday of Advent tells the longing for the Messiah and calls the community to wait expectantly, both for the birth of the Christ child and for his reign at the end of time.
- The second Sunday of Advent retells the story of John the Baptist and his summons of all persons to repent and bear fruit worthy of that repentance.
- The third Sunday of Advent recalls the relationship between John and Jesus and reminds the church that the Messiah is at hand.
- And the fourth Sunday of Advent reminds the church that the birth of Mary's son is the fulfillment of all God's promises. And Mary becomes the archetype of how persons should respond to God's favor.

Such readings encourage the congregation to remember the severe clash of cultures between God's realm and human society. Joy and thanksgiving do not immediately appear when stores begin their Christmas sales after Thanksgiving. Rather, the joy of Christmas must be preceded by a time of preparation and confession.

The classic Advent hymn by Charles Wesley, "Come, Thou Long-Expected Jesus" shares clearly the message of the time:

>Come, thou long-expected Jesus,
>born to set thy people free;
>from our fears and sins release us,
>let us find our rest in thee.
>Israel's strength and consolation,
>hope of all the earth thou art;
>dear desire of every nation,
>joy of every longing heart.
>
>Born thy people to deliver,
>born a child and yet a King,
>born to reign in us forever,
>now thy gracious kingdom bring.
>By thine own eternal spirit
>rule in all our hearts alone;
>by thine all-sufficient merit,
>raise us to thy glorious throne.

Advent is an excellent time for worship and evangelism. The sanctuary clothed in purple, blue, and dark paraments; the Advent wreath; and other signs remind the congregation of darkness and light. Revivals and preaching missions would be appropriate, particularly as they focus on the need for the Messiah. Music ought to explore the more mellow and minor keys of human existence. The "Canticle of Mary" (199) can become the paradigm of all our responses to God. Do not minimize the anticipation of the Messiah by singing Christmas carols too early. Encourage prayers of confession and invite persons to come forward to the altar to pray. In summary, focus on the need of all persons and every community for the in-breaking of God's love. Identify the needs—peace within each person and among all nations, repentance from sins of commission or omission, and fortitude to continue the good fight. Only when needs have been clearly and sharply identified will there be an openness to the riches of God's gift in Christ Jesus.

In addition, two special programs during Advent may help expand your congregation's awareness of the gospel's call not only to personal devotion, but also to social reformation. The "Alternatives" ministry (P. O. Box 429, Ellenwood, GA 30049) offers these two programs: "Whose Birthday Is It, Anyway?" and "The Light Shines in the Darkness." Both programs offer meaningful celebrations of Advent and Christmas, which remind a congregation that Christ's coming was good news to the poor and those oppressed by war, and call a congregation to support this struggle.

In summary, observe Advent in a way that encourages the community to reflect on its own need for the coming One, so that the arrival of Christmas comes with clearer understanding and great celebration.

## CHRISTMAS

"The grace of God has appeared for the salvation of all people. God's grace teaches us to reject godless ways and worldly desires, and to live temperately, justly, and devoutly in the present age, while we are awaiting our blessed hope—when the glory of our great God and Savior Christ Jesus will appear. It is Christ who gave up life for us, to set us free from all wickedness and to make us eager to do good, a pure people who are Christ's very own."

Titus 2:11-14<br>
Christmas Eve<br>
Year B

Christmas—with lights, songs, presents, and praise—reminds the church that God is in the midst of the broken world. Now is the time to celebrate the Incarnation: God becoming flesh that our flesh might become divine.

In too many congregations, the twelve days of Christmas are a low season: low attendance, low energy, low expectations. Yet what a stark contrast to the very nature of the season:

> Joy to the world, the Lord is come!
> Let earth receive her King;
> let every heart prepare him room,
> and heaven and nature sing.
>
> Joy to the world! the Savior reigns!
> Let all their songs employ;
> while fields and floods, rocks, hills, and plains
> repeat the sounding joy.
>
> No more let sins and sorrows grow,
> nor thorns infest the ground;
> he comes to make his blessings flow
> far as the curse is found.
>
> He rules the world with truth and grace,
> and makes the nations prove
> the glories of his righteousness,
> and wonders of his love.
>
> Isaac Watts

Now is the time to bring out your finest paraments, robes, albs, and banners. Light every candle you can find. Sing the Christmas carols over and over again. Encourage the children to act out the Christmas story. Proclaim that God has sent forth a light in the midst of the darkness. Be open to the wide variety of Christmas tales that may be shared during this season. Stories such as "The Little Drummer Boy" and "A Christmas Story" are faithful to the Christmas message and capture the imagination of children and adults. Concentrate on prayers of thanksgiving, with the people standing to pray. Celebrate the Lord's Supper with joy. Too many congregations believe the holy meal to be a penitential act rather than a joyful celebration of Christ's continuing presence with all faithful souls.

The Day of Epiphany is the climax of the cycle and the final day of the season of Christmas. In the Western church, a primary focus is on the coming of the magi, while in the Eastern church, the baptism of Christ has prominence. Whichever direction your church chooses to go, this day should be an important day of celebration and proclamation of God's love. Light the candles. Baptize persons. Sing the "Canticle of Simeon" (225). Help your whole congregation reaffirm the Baptismal Covenant. John

Wesley regularly observed services of the new year called "Watch Night" or "Covenant Renewal," either of which would be appropriate models for congregations today.

## Lent/Easter/Pentecost

Throughout Lent, the membership/confirmation class of the Avery Parish met. Together the youth studied the lectionary readings for each week and discussed their meanings. Together they prayed and helped at the local emergency clothing center. On Easter morning, they led in the Sunrise Service. Throughout the Easter season they continued their reading of the lectionary and prepared to make a decision about church membership. And on the Day of Pentecost, several, though not all, came forward to affirm the Baptismal Covenant and join the church. So those who received God's Word were baptized, and there were added that day about four souls. And they devoted themselves to the church's teaching and fellowship, to the breaking of bread, and to prayers and service.

The journey of these new members of the church has been repeated for two thousand years. From the earliest days of the church, Christians have waited with great devotion on Christ's death and resurrection. It became an early custom of the church to prepare for Easter with a season of confession, fasting, and prayer. This time provided an occasion for persons to renew themselves for the great holy feast days of Easter by recognizing their dependency on God. And then in the fifty days of Easter, as Christ's resurrection initiated a new creation, so persons joined the community of faith.

### LENT

"Blow the trumpet in Zion; sound the alarm on my holy mountain! Let all who dwell in the land tremble, for the day of Yahweh is coming!

Yes, it is near a day of darkness, of gloom; a day of dense cloud spreading like soot across the hills. . . .

But Yahweh says, "Now, even now, come back to me; return with all your heart, with fasting and weeping and mourning. But show your grief in broken hearts, and not by clothes of mourning.

Turn back again Yahweh to your God, who is gracious and full of motherly compassion, slow to anger and abounding in loyalty, and ready to renounce punishment. . . .

Blow the trumpet in Zion! Proclaim a fast and call a sacred assembly.
Gather the people, and summon the congregation. Assemble the elders and gather the children, even nursing infants.
Bid the bridegroom leave his room and the bride her chamber.
Between the portico and the altar let the priests, ministers of Yahweh, stand weeping, and say,
'Spare your people, Yahweh, your own people!'"

Joel 2;1-2,12-17a<br>Ash Wednesday<br>Years A, B, C

Lent is a season of forty days, not counting Sundays, which begins on Ash Wednesday and ends on Holy Saturday. During this period of preparation for Easter, persons may observe a season of spiritual devotion including prayer, gift-giving, scripture reading, and fasting. Each year, Lent helps people anticipate not the crucifixion of Christ but Jesus' resurrection and triumph over sin and death and their significance for all creation.

Ash Wednesday begins the season. A service in the evening with an imposition of ashes marks persons with a sign of mortality. Evangelistically, persons cannot receive the gift of life until they recognize the reality of sin and death.

Every year the first Sunday of Lent focuses on the temptations of Jesus. There is no better time for persons to be reminded of their own temptations with the resulting successes and failures. Then, in Year A of the Common Lectionary, the Gospel readings focus on divine encounter—between Jesus and Nicodemus, the woman at the well, the man born blind, and Lazarus. In Year B, the focus is on Jesus' judgment of Peter and the Temple, and the present and future time of accounting. Finally, Year C focuses on the call to repentance in each of the readings, including the parable of the prodigal son and the story of Jesus with the adulterous woman.

Lent reaches its climax during Holy Week. This week tells the whole mystery of crucifixion and resurrection and invites participation by the entire community. Passion/Palm Sunday involves all persons. Just as a congregation shouts "Hosanna" in the 'Service of the Palms,' it then becomes the crowd that shouts "Crucify him" in the 'Service of the Word.' Each service of Holy Week helps build anticipation to Holy Thursday. In this full service, persons confess sins, hear the Word read and proclaimed, wash one anothers' feet, receive Holy Communion, strip the church, and extinguish all lights. The journey to Golgotha is complete.

Each year, the classic Lenten hymn calls to mind the personal implications of observing this season:

> Alas! and did my Savior bleed,
> and did my Sovereign die?
> Would he devote that sacred head
> for sinners such as I?
>
> Was it for crimes that I have done,
> he groaned upon the tree?
> Amazing pity! Grace unknown!
> And love beyond degree!
>
> Well might the sun in darkness hide,
> and shut its glories in,
> when God, the mighty maker, died
> for his own creature's sin.
>
> Thus might I hide my blushing face
> while his dear cross appears;
> dissolve my heart in thankfulness,
> and melt mine eyes to tears.
>
> But drops of tears can ne'er repay
> the debt of love I owe.
> Here, Lord, I give myself away;
> 'Tis all that I can do."
> "Alas, and Did My Savior Bleed," Johan Hermann

Lent is possibly the best time of the year for services that are clearly evangelistic. Revival and preaching services may develop the themes of the season and speak to a specific community. The quality of the sanctuary setting may be dark and austere, through the use of such signs as a cross draped in black cloth. Prayer should focus on extended occasions for silent and vocal confessions, and petitions. Encourage persons to come and kneel for prayer or indicate another reflective posture.

Another approach to Lent can be found in "The Cost of Discipleship." Produced by "Alternatives," this resource may enable your congregation to follow Jesus by taking up the cross in our broken world. This program pushes congregations beyond a pietistic understanding of Easter to a more holistic participation in Christ's triumph over all the forces of Satan.

Now, as the congregation has come to the cross and rock-covered tomb, the stage is set for Easter.

## EASTER

[To the gathering assembled at the home of Cornelius, the Roman centurion]

"Peter said, "The truth, I now realize, is that God does not show partiality, but accepts from any nation those who are God fearing and who do what is right. This is the message God sent to the people of Israel, proclaiming the good news of peace through Jesus Christ, who is Lord of all. You yourselves already know about the recent happenings throughout Judea, beginning in Galilee after the baptism that John proclaimed. You know how God anointed Jesus of Nazareth with the Holy Spirit and with power. And because God was with him, Jesus went about doing good and healing all who were oppressed by the devil.

"Now I, and those with me, can witness to all that Jesus did throughout the countryside of Judea and in Jerusalem itself. He was killed by hanging on a tree. But this is the one God raised to life on the third day, who appeared, not to all the people, but to us who had already been chosen by God to be witnesses, who ate and drank with Jesus after he rose from the dead.

"Jesus commanded us to proclaim to the people and to testify that he is the one appointed by God to be judge of the living and the dead. Jesus is the one about whom all the prophets testify, that everyone who trusts in him receives forgiveness of sins through his name."

Acts 10:34-43
The Day of Easter
Years A, B, C.

Easter is the most holy and joyful time of the year. The services of Easter Day, and the whole celebration of the great "Fifty Days," should tell of God's mighty acts in Christ Jesus who destroyed all the powers and principalities of evil. This time should be the highest time of the year for your congregation.

Throughout the season, focus on the grace of God that conquers all. On Easter Day, declare the resurrection through word, song, and action. Light every candle and display the finest paraments. Serve the Lord's

# The Christian Year

Supper as the "Eucharist," a thanksgiving meal that we share with the risen Christ. As in the early church, receive new persons into the community through the Baptismal Covenant.

Throughout Easter, declare how God demonstrates the resurrection in the church, the Body of Christ. Tell a people who sat through darkness that Jesus Christ is the good shepherd, the way, the truth, the life, and the vine. Finally, remind the people that God is still at work in the church through the Holy Spirit, as most visibly demonstrated at Pentecost. In A Service of Baptismal Reaffirmation, let the waters of Christ wash off the ashes imposed on Ash Wednesday. Easter is a season of pentecostal power in its fullest sense. Declare it as good news.

Encourage the people to sing: "Come, Ye Faithful, Raise the Strain":

> Come, ye faithful, raise the strain
> of triumphant gladness;
> God hath brought forth Israel
> into joy from sadness;
> loosed from Pharaoh's bitter yoke
> Jacob's sons and daughters,
> led them with unmoistened foot
> through the Red Sea waters.
>
> 'Tis the spring of souls today;
> Christ hath burst his prison,
> and from three days' sleep in death
> as a sun hath risen;
> all the winter of our sins,
> long and dark, is flying
> from his light, to whom we give
> laud and praise undying.
>
> Neither might the gates of death,
> nor the tomb's dark portal,
> nor the watchers, nor the seal
> hold thee as a mortal;
> but today amidst the twelve
> thou didst stand, bestowing
> that thy peace which evermore
> passeth human knowing.
>
> "Alleluia!" now we cry
> to our King immortal,

who, triumphant, burst the bars
of the tomb's dark portal;
"Alleluia!" with the Son,
God the Father praising,
"Alleluia!" yet again
to the Spirit raising.
John of Damascus

Worship and evangelism at their best both tell the good news. The best good news the church has to share is that Jesus Christ is alive and present in every Christian and in the community of faith. Every sign and action of the church needs to declare this good news in every moment throughout Easter. Avoid talking about sin and death. Instead, proclaim with joy what God has done for all creation. Preaching should be optimistic; music should be uplifting; prayer should be thankful. Encourage persons to stand for prayer and lift their hands toward heaven. Pass the peace of God with one another. Celebrate the Eucharist frequently.

## Ordinary Time

"And Jesus went about all the towns and villages, teaching in their synagogues and proclaiming the good news of God's Kingdom, and curing all kinds of sickness and disease. When Jesus saw the crowds, he felt compassion for them, because they were harrassed and helpless, like sheep without a shepherd.

Then Jesus said to his disciples, "The harvest is plentiful, but the workers are few; so ask the Lord of the harvest to send out workers into the harvest field."

Jesus summoned the twelve disciples, and gave them authority to cast out evil spirits and to heal all kinds of sickness and disease. These twelve Jesus sent out with the instructions: "Don't go among the gentiles, nor enter every Samaritan town. Go instead to the lost sheep of the people of Israel. Go proclaiming, 'The kingdom of heaven is at hand!' Heal the sick, raise the dead, cleanse the leprous, cast out demons. Freely you have received, so now freely give."

Matthew 9:35; 10:1,5-8a<br>Season after Pentecost<br>Proper 6<br>Year A

# The Christian Year

After the two great cycles of Advent/Christmas/Epiphany and Lent/Easter/Pentecost, the church moves into "Ordinary Time" or the Season after Pentecost. Throughout Ordinary Time, the Common Lectionary uses scripture in a distinctive way. While from Advent through Pentecost the Gospel reading of each day determines the other lessons, in Ordinary Time the readings from the Gospels, Epistles, and Old Testament are each read sequentially. They are not, except in the broadest terms, linked together. Therefore, pastors may choose to concentrate for a time solely on the Gospel readings, then move to the Epistle, and then to the Old Testament. This allows time for a concentrated emphasis on one book of the Bible rather than on a broad theme. The following discussion describes how this process works.

In Year A, the Gospel of Matthew controls the lectionary. Understanding Christ as the fulfillment of the law and prophets, Matthew speaks to the community of faith. The emphasis is on the presence of Christ in the life of the church. One implication for worship and evangelism is to focus on the community of faith as a witness of and to grace. Offer good news to the members of your church and call them to be bearers of the good news. For example, the Sermon on the Mount is as an invitation to receive and offer hope to a community and world distanced from God.

Also in Year A, the Old Testament lessons concentrate on the patriarchs and Moses, from the call of Abraham to the death of Moses, plus Ruth. The evangelistic opportunities are dramatic. Such readings may call a community to establish a new covenant with God. The journey from Egypt to the Promised Land parallels many lives. And Ruth's faithfulness becomes a model for all to follow.

Romans and First Thessalonians in Year A are read consecutively. Just as Martin Luther and Karl Barth initiated revivals by beginning with the Book of Romans, so might your church. First Thessalonians' focus on the end-time offers materials for serious study.

In Year B of the lectionary, the Gospel of Mark prevails. Focusing on the person and work of Jesus Christ, Mark uncovers through the messianic secret of the passion and resurrection of Jesus the radical implications for all humanity. The crisp and clear message of Mark makes the good news plain. For example, Peter's confession in Mark 8 is a clear model for all followers of the way.

The Old Testament in Year B concentrates on David, from his anointing to his death. Proclamation of this extended narrative may enable your congregation to experience the ebb and flow of David's relationship with God.

The Epistles in Year B—Second Corinthians, Ephesians, James, and

Hebrews—all are worthy of a series of services focusing on the nature of Christian community and life.

Year C of the lectionary concentrates on the Gospel of Luke. Luke's cosmic vision understands Jesus Christ as the savior of all creation. The ministry of Christ, marked by moments of reconciliation, calls forth followers to tell the good news. Passages like the parables of recovery (the lost coin, the lost sheep, and the prodigal son) are typical of the Gospel.

The Old Testament readings in Year C focus on the Elijah-Elisha story, from Solomon's dedication of the Temple to the death of Elisha. The minor prophets are also emphasized. Worship may center on the relationship of God with the community of faith, emphasizing both hope and judgment.

The Epistle readings from Galatians, Colossians, Hebrews, Philemon, First and Second Timothy, and Second Thessalonians narrate life in the early community of faith. Any one of these books is worthy of focus.

Again, during Ordinary Time, do not be concerned with finding a common theme in all the lessons appointed for any Sunday. Deal with each scripture separately. Choose the one most appropriate to the congregation. Then design services of worship that are centered on the Word and that call forth faithful discipleship.

## Special Services

Throughout the Christian year, in addition to the two great cycles and ordinary time, there are particular occasions in the lives of individuals and communities that offer unique opportunities for worship with an evangelistic focus. Each occasion should be chosen as an event to offer God's grace to persons and congregations.

In Florida, one congregation observes a yearly service of "reconciliation of inactives." During the fall, the pastor visits each inactive member or household of his congregation. Pastoral counseling takes place as persons describe the individuals or the occasions that led to their "backsliding" from the faith. Then, on the Sunday before the first Sunday of Advent, the congregation receives back into its midst those persons who wish to become active again in the life of the congregation. The service includes confession by individuals and the whole congregation, followed by words of forgiveness, and then the passing of the peace.

> "Dying, Christ destroyed our death.
> Rising, Christ restored our life.
> Christ will come again in glory."
> Introduction to *A Service of Death and Resurrection*

Funerals and memorial services offer opportunities of grace. Effective funeral services invoke both the reality of death and the reality of the resurrection for all who believe. Every pastor has stories about how persons have been brought back into the community of faith following sensitive and powerful funeral liturgies and sermons. The goal is not to make a funeral an occasion to "repent, for tomorrow you may die," but an opportunity to offer hope in the midst of death.

Weddings may become powerful testimonies for the active and creative love of God. When couples, families, and friends come to the church for a wedding, the happy occasion should be the opportunity to express the nature of Christian commitment and all the blessings it may bestow. The pastor and the congregation should help persons who are newly married persons be incorporated and strengthened in the community of faith. The same is also true for the families of the couple. Increasingly, the linking of services of Christian marriage with the sacrament of Holy Communion are strong public testimonies. And when couples reaffirm their marriage vows, as happens frequently on major wedding anniversaries, God's on-going grace is recognized and couples, families, and congregations are renewed.

Vacation Bible school assemblies are ideal occasions for linking worship and evangelism. Many children, along with their parents, who are not active in congregations, come to these church educational opportunities. Use the opening or closing assembly to sing familiar hymns, especially those geared toward children, to read scripture, and to share the gospel. Such informal worship is attractive to non-practicing persons and allows people, dressed as they are and being who they are, to worship God.

New Year's Eve was a night of high celebration in Atlanta. For weeks night clubs, hotels, and bars advertised their parties and spectacular shows. At Norcross United Methodist Church, the congregation scheduled a midnight communion service. Since the service was competing against all the other festivities, not many persons were expected. Yet at midnight, 200 persons came. Together they sang hymns, heard the scripture read and preached, and offered prayers of thanksgiving for the year past and prayers of intercession for the year to come. Then they received the holy meal. As many commented at the close of the service, this church offered an alternative to a night of debauchery. Like John Wesley's Watch Night Services of years gone by, the church offered an alternative to the excesses of secular society.

Youth Sunday at Hudson United Methodist Church was an evangelistic service. For weeks the full youth group planned a service that reflected their faith. They chose hymns they loved and prayers they had written. They sang in the choir and took up the offering. And they invited their friends. Taken seriously by the congregation, the youth took their responsibility seriously and led a powerful worship service. Years later many of these youth, now adults, are still active in the church. Remember, worship is the work of the people and should be planned with and by the whole congregation. Take your youth seriously and let them, on a regular basis, offer God's call and be encouraged to respond.

Finally, four other programs, offered by the General Board of Discipleship, also may be considered as events during ordinary time: the "Key Event Celebration," the "Lay Witness Mission," the "New Life Mission," and the "New World Mission." A "Key Event Celebration" focuses on the key event in the Christian faith, that is, Jesus Christ. During three phases, participants discuss basic questions of the faith, celebrate the incarnation, crucifixion, resurrection, and Pentecost, and communicate the good news. A "Lay Witness Mission" is a weekend experience designed to help persons renew their commitment to Christ and to gain a sense of belonging to a community of redemption. The three phases of the "New Life Mission" focus on gathering in homes, inviting new persons, and understanding God's grace in one's life. The three phases of the "New World Mission" focus on global awareness, the reign of God, and developing outreach ministries with "Missioners" and Christian leaders from around the world. Contact the Section on Evangelism of the General Board of Discipleship for further information.

## Summary

By following the Christian year, your congregation can initiate persons into the family of Christ. The Christian year provides the broad groundwork upon which persons and communities can build their own lives. By taking seriously God's dramatic intervention into human history, you can help lives be formed in divine ways. The journey of the congregation from anticipation (Advent) to full empowerment (Pentecost) thus becomes the model for personal commitment.

# 6. PLANNING FOR WORSHIP AND EVANGELISM

This meeting occurs in every United Methodist congregation that is serious about worship and evangelism. The pastor has gathered with several key laypersons in the church. The laity might include the chairs of the worship and evangelism committees, the church musician(s), the head usher and greeter, and others with particular interests in this ministry. Together they create an agenda for their congregation to strengthen worship and evangelism.

How do you form such a group? What goes on your agenda? How will you work together? Strong leadership, good teaching, extensive plans, congregational support, and evaluation and refinement are all critical aspects of planning for worship and evangelism.

## Strong Leadership

At First United Methodist Church in Charlotte, a growing congregation in the downtown area, pastor Harold Bales attends regularly only one committee of the church: the worship committee. He recognizes that effective evangelism depends fundamentally on effective services of worship.

For both worship and evangelism to be effective, the leaders of your congregation must demonstrate strong leadership. Leaders must lead. If they do not, this book and all your plans will be in vain. But if they take responsibility, God will use them in your church.

The primary responsibility for effective worship and evangelism belongs to the pastor of your congregation. In particular, the pastor should:

- Emphasize worship and evangelism and how they can work together.
- Recruit, through your nominations committee and through special invitation, persons with particular skills and interests in worship and evangelism.

- Train persons in worship and evangelism.
- Guide these persons to integrate and enhance both worship and evangelism.

Such pastoral leadership is critical if you wish to succeed.

Yet effective worship and evangelism also depend on a solid core of dedicated persons—lay, diaconal, and ordained—who plan together in these two areas. If your congregation depends solely on the work of the pastor in charge, then neither worship nor evangelism will work effectively. Worship is the work of the people and evangelism is the responsibility of the whole community of faith.

In your congregation there are persons with particular skills in worship and evangelism. Your musicians, choir director, song leader, choir members, ushers, acolytes, altar guild members, worship committee members, Communion stewards, and others have been gifted with special abilities. Likewise, your evangelism committee, church visitors, neighborhood shepherds, greeters, and others have been blessed with distinctive skills. When your congregation gathers all these persons together and sets them on the task to offer God's grace through worship, wonderful things will happen.

The critical first step in effective planning is assembling a core leadership team in your local church. Too often, worship and evangelism are the responsibility of distinct groups of leaders who rarely work together. The key to enabling worship and evangelism to be mutually supportive is to have key leadership work and plan together toward the common goal of offering God's love to your whole community.

## Good Teaching

At Pisgah United Methodist Church, members of the evangelism committee and worship committee met together in January at Fred and Lil Conner's home. The goal was to plan for worship during Lent and Easter and to determine how these services would enhance evangelism. But first, the committee members talked together about what worship and evangelism meant to them.

When you have assembled your key leaders together, the next stage of planning involves teaching your team about both worship and evangelism. Too often, agendas compete and conflict with each other. To avoid such a struggle, work with all the persons and explain the nature and practice of effective worship and evangelism.

# Planning for Worship and Evangelism

Several resources will aid you as you train this team. You may wish to order a copy of this book for each member of your committee or at least one copy for the chair of your worship committee and one for the chair of your evangelism committee. Also, for your worship chair, you may order *Guidelines for Leaders in the Local Church: 1989-1992: Worship* and Hoyt Hickman's *Planning Worship Each Week* or *A Primer for Church Worship.* These are popular and pragmatic resources for laity in the local church. For your evangelism chair, you may order: *Guidelines for Leaders in the Local Church: 1989-1992: Evangelism.*

Another excellent resource for worship and evangelism is found not in written form, but in other congregations. Every pastor and all key leaders should visit the worship services of other churches in your community. Visit those churches with other worship traditions and congregations that serve a different social or ethnic group. Evaluate their worship. What is effective? What ministers to the needs of that congregation? What can you learn? Every illustration in this book comes from experiences of visiting congregations and learning from them. This can be true for you. After you have gleaned information from other churches, you can use your insights to teach others.

An ideal time for such training is at a retreat. Take the team to a nearby camp, another church, or other place apart and spend time together. An outsider may be invited to help guide your group process. Plan times of worship, not for demonstration, but for the individuals and the whole group to hear and respond to God. Evaluate the worship and the evangelism in your local church. Emphasize what your church does well. Study together a book or article on either worship or evangelism. Make lists of what you wish to accomplish. Plan ahead. (See the next section.) At the end of your time, worship together as you commit yourselves to a common ministry in a Covenant Renewal Service or a Reaffirmation of the Baptismal Covenant.

This period of training is an important yet often underused tool for planning. Effective planning depends on a solid group of dedicated persons who know each other, trust each other, support each other, and are willing to deny individual concerns for the greater good. When you train your committee for this task, you are over halfway home.

## Extensive Plans

At Fred and Lil's house, the Pisgah planning team decided to coordinate the services of Lent and Easter with its evangelistic efforts. The Ash Wednesday Service would call people to repentance. The services of Lent would call for recommitment. Persons not active in church would be prayed for and visited. A revival would be held during Holy Week. The services of Easter would celebrate God's gracious acts in the community. Leaders were chosen, responsibilities were assigned, and the work began.

Your leadership team must move from commitment to a task roughly defined to a specific ministry clearly outlined. At your planning retreat, plan! You may wish to use Hoyt Hickman's *Planning Worship Each Week* as an outline for your work. To aid in the task of planning, the following model may work in your church. The first five steps should be taken by the pastor. These steps require a brief time of looking beyond the planning retreat.

1. *Plan ahead.* Set aside at least half a day to plan. Using a calendar, plan in advance for a whole season of the year at a time, at least eight weeks before the season begins. For example, no later than October 1, plan for the Advent/Christmas/Epiphany cycle: the First Sunday of Advent to the Day of Epiphany. No later than January 1, plan for the Lent/Easter/Pentecost cycle: Ash Wednesday to the Day of Pentecost. And no later than April 1, plan for June, July, and August.

    Determine which services will be held during that season. Include every Sunday and then add any special services such as Christmas Eve, Ash Wednesday, or a revival or preaching mission.

    Use the model worksheet in this book (p. 75) and make one worksheet for every service. Write in the date of the service. Include the day of the Christian year. Make a file folder for each service. Start collecting all the resources to use for the planning of this service of worship.

2. *Choose scripture lessons.* Select which Bible passages are the foundation for each service of worship. The Common Lectionary—a three-year cycle of selected Old Testament, Psalm, Epistle, and New Testament readings—is one source of scrip-

ture readings. A primary advantage of the lectionary is that it makes planning ahead simple.

Or, the pastor may choose scripture based on a theme or themes for the whole season. You may decide to use one book of the Bible and work through the book during a particular season. If you use either of these two ways, be sure to cover both the Old Testament and New Testament over a period of time.

Write down the lessons on the worksheet, and read the lessons for each service.

Select the primary lesson that will be the cornerstone of the service. The lesson may be from the Old or New Testament and will guide the whole shape of the service.

3. *Choose the sermon focus.* The sermon links the Bible with the people and the church. The sermon focus—the basic image, thrust, statement, or impact that guides the sermon—will give direction to the service. The preacher needs to ask, "How does the scripture affect me and this congregation?", "Where does the scripture challenge?", "Where does the scripture comfort?", and "What responses does the scripture call forth?"

Write the sermon focus in a short, declarative sentence. Even though the sermon may not be prepared for several weeks, the sermon focus will prove invaluable to the preacher, musician(s), and worship planning team. With the sermon focus in mind, the preacher may collect sermon ideas in the weeks ahead. Place those ideas in the worksheet file folders.

4. *Communion, special emphasis, or special service?* Determine if a service has a special emphasis. Is there to be communion, a baptism, an installation of officers, a dedication of hymnals, or anything else that would affect the service? Write it down.

5. *Schedule a planning retreat.* Schedule a retreat with the musician(s) and the worship/evangelism planning team. Remember, schedule the meeting at least eight weeks before a season begins.

6. *Prepare for your planning retreat.* Duplicate the worksheets for each service in the whole season—complete with date, day in the Christian year, scripture lessons and primary lesson, sermon focus, and special emphasis. Distribute the sheets to all members of the planning team.

The musician(s), pastor, and other worship planners should prepare suggestions concerning hymns, anthem(s), other worship leaders, and visuals.

At the planning meeting, do the following:

7. *Select hymns.* Together, choose hymns for the services. In general, all the hymns should reflect and enhance the scripture of the day, the sermon focus, or the service emphasis. For example, the first hymn may be a hymn of praise, the second may be related to the sermon, and the third may be a response to the Word, a Communion hymn, or a hymn of sending forth.

   Choose both familiar and new hymns. While most hymns chosen for the services will be familiar to the congregation, you should also choose some unfamiliar hymns to expand and deepen the congregation's experience of worship. You may choose at least one new hymn each season.

   One way to introduce an unfamiliar hymn text is to set it to a familiar tune. The metrical index in the back of the hymnal can help you determine what other tunes are likely to fit the words you want to sing. Other options can be found in *The Hymns of The United Methodist Hymnal.* Write down the hymn titles and tune names.

8. *Choose anthem(s), service/Communion music, and instrumental music.* Based on the scripture lessons, sermon focus, or the service emphasis, the musician(s) and pastor should work together to create an environment of sound that enhances worship. For example, the psalm of the day may be sung.

   Do not be afraid of being creative. Involve the congregation as much as possible. After all, everyone is a participant in worship. Choose singers and instrumentalists. Contact them well in advance. Write down your decisions.

9. *Select other worship leaders.* Lay liturgists, readers, acolytes, Communion servers, ushers, and greeters are designated and trained. Other participants—dancers, mimes, and other artists—should be chosen. As leaders are chosen, include persons of all ages and conditions. Children, youth, and adults of all ages love to participate if asked and prepared. Persons with handicapping conditions can add greatly to the whole congregation's

# Planning for Worship and Evangelism

worship. Involve members of the evangelism work area.

Write down the names and contact the people well in advance. When particular persons are chosen for a special service, give them a copy of the worksheet for the service for their preparations.

10. *Determine visuals.* After the scripture, sermon focus, hymns, music, and leaders have been chosen, determine the visual environment of worship.

    Select the liturgical color(s). Work with the flower coordinator, altar guild, or florist to select appropriate flowers or table settings. Plan to unwrap the Advent wreath, dust off the Chrismons, construct a rugged cross, purchase a Christ candle, order a new Communion cup and plate, or place an order for bread. Assign responsibilities.

    Look again at the church's paraments, the choir's robes, the pastor's robe/alb and stoles. Which will go best with the scripture at each service? Write this information down.

# A Worksheet for Planning a Worship Service

Date _____    Day in the Church Year _____

Scriptures:    Liturgical Color _____
First _____    Will there be Communion? _____
Psalm _____    Special Emphasis or Special Service:
Second _____    _____
Gospel _____    _____
Sermon Focus:

Hymns: _____ _____
         _____ _____
         _____ _____

Anthems: _____

Service/Communion Music: _____
_____
_____

Instrumental Music: _____
_____

Psalmody: _____
Lay Liturgists/Readers: _____
Acolytes: _____
Other Participants: _____
_____

Visuals: _____
Other Information: _____

Do not stop when you have completed the worship planning sheets. Go back through these services and determine how your evangelistic ministry fits this worship pattern. For example:

- Are there persons we have left out of these services? If so, how can we plan with special audiences in mind?
- Is there a need for another special service or services such as a revival or an additional service on Sunday or another day?
- Are these particular services times when members need to invite friends, neighbors, and coworkers?
- What other locations ought to be considered for worship services?
- How can our services be advertised?
- What invitations ought to be offered in each service?
- What responses are you prepared for?
- What role can the evangelism committee play in these services? Do you need more greeters, visitors, or healing teams?

Write all of this information down. Then choose leaders and assign responsibilities.

Not all the suggestions offered in this book can or should be used in your congregation. They describe practical and useful ideas gleaned from many congregations. The pastor and worship/evangelism committee must decide together what plans to make and how to implement them. It is better to do one new thing well to attract persons to your church (from Chapter One) than to do several things poorly. If your leaders are sensitive, prayerful, wise, and reverent, they can make significant reforms in your worship and evangelism.

## Congregational Support

After our meeting at Fred and Lil's home, members of the worship/evangelism committee took reports back to their families and Sunday school classes. The parish newsletter detailed their plans, and the committee chair reminded the congregation each week during the time of announcements. By Ash Wednesday attendance increased, and the Holy Week revival had the largest attendance ever. Many persons recommitted themselves to God.

Planning for worship and evangelism demands that the work of a worship/evangelism committee be shared and owned by the congregation. Your whole congregation should know what you are planning to do and how its people may be involved.

The avenues of communication are many. Make your plans known through Sunday school classes and other small groups in your congregation. Talk about them in the sermons. Hold a special session for the choir members, acolytes, ushers, greeters, and others involved in the process. Pray together, using *Pray and Grow: Evangelism Prayer Ministries*, by Terry Teykl. Publish your plans in your newsletter and bulletin. Advise the official bodies of your congregation—your Administrative Council or your Council on Ministries and Administrative Board—and ask them to adopt your plans. Everyone in your congregation should know what you are planning, why you are planning as you are, and how they may participate. Only then will worship become the work of the people and evangelism the responsibility of each Christian.

## Evaluation and Refinement

During the summer following the Lent-to-Pentecost emphasis, the committee gathered at Pisgah Church to evaluate its work. In the context of good work, members of the worship/evangelism committee realized that it could have done better work. They did not advertise well in the community. They did not sufficiently prepare the revival preacher. And they did not follow through on all the plans. So they began work on the services for the following year.

The final, and often forgotten, stage of planning is evaluation and refinement. Never will all your dreams be realized. Rather, every success and failure offers insights into how to share God's love more fully the next time. Therefore, during and after every major effort critique your efforts, be thankful for your successes, and amend your mistakes. The hope of the Christian faith is that God takes us, broken and incomplete, and makes us whole and complete.

## Conclusion

And Jesus went about all the towns and villages, teaching in their synagogues and proclaiming the good news of God's kingdom, and curing all kinds of sickness and disease. When Jesus saw the crowds, he felt compassion for them, because they were harassed and helpless, like sheep without a shepherd. Then he said to his disciples,

"The harvest is plentiful, but the workers are few; so ask the Lord of the harvest to send out workers into his harvest field."
Matthew 9:35-38

> A charge to keep I have,
> a God to glorify,
> a never-dying soul to save,
> and fit it for the sky.
>
> To serve the present age,
> my calling to fufill;
> O may it all my powers engage
> to do my Master's will!
> Charles Wesley, "A Charge to Keep I Have"

# BIBLIOGRAPHY

Anderson, J. D. and Jones, E. E., *Ministry of the Laity* (Harper and Row, 1986).

Armstrong, R. S., *The Pastor—Evangelist in Worship* (Westminster, 1986).

Bales, Harold K., *A Comprehensive Plan for Evangelism* (Discipleship Resources, 1981).

Braden, Suzanne, *The First Year: Incorporating New Members into the Congregation* (Discipleship Resources, 1987).

Callahan, Kennon L., *Twelve Keys to an Effective Church* (Harper and Row, 1983).

*God's Children in Worship Kit* (Discipleship Resources, 1988).

*Guidelines for Leaders in the Local Church, 1989-1992: Evangelism* (Abingdon, 1988).

*Guidelines for Leaders in the Local Church, 1989-1992: Worship* (Abingdon, 1988).

Harding, Joe, *Growth Plus Worship Attendance Crusade Kit* (Discipleship Resources, 1988).

Hartman, Warren, *Five Audiences* (Abingdon, 1987).

Hickman, Hoyt, *Companion to the Book of Services* (Abingdon, 1988).

———. *The Worship Resources of The United Methodist Hymnal* (Abingdon, 1989).

———. *Planning Worship Each Week* (Discipleship Resources, 1988).

———. *Holy Communion* (Abingdon, 1987).

Hickman, Hoyt, *A Primer for Church Worship* (Abingdon, 1984).

Hickman, Saliers, Stookey, White, *Handbook of the Christian Year* (Abingdon, 1986).

Johnson, Ken, *Ushering and Greeting* (Discipleship Resources, 1989).

*An Invitation from Your United Methodist Friends* (Discipleship Resources, 1984).

Kerr, H. T. and Mulder, J. M., *Conversions* (Eerdmans, 1983).

Langford, T.A. and Jones, B. S., *The Worship Handbook* (Discipleship Resources, 1984).

Martin, O. Dean, *Invite: Preaching for Response* (Discipleship Resources, 1987).

Morris, George E., *The Mystery and Meaning of Christian Conversion* (Discipleship Resources, 1981).

"Net Results," a monthly periodical on evangelism (5001 Avenue N, Lubbock, TX 79412).

Sanchez, Diana, *The Hymns of The United Methodist Hymnal* (Abingdon, 1989).

Teykl, Terry, *Pray and Grow* (Discipleship Resources, 1988).

Wagner, James, *Blessed to Be a Blessing* (The Upper Room, 1980).

Ward, Richard, *Reading Scripture Aloud* (Discipleship Resources, 1989).

Williams, Michael, *Preaching Pilgrims* (Discipleship Resources, 1988).

Willimon, Will, *Remember Who You Are* (The Upper Room, 1980).

———. *Sunday Dinner* (The Upper Room, 1981).

Wiltse, David, *Designing the Sunday Bulletin* (Discipleship Resources, 1983).